Picture Brides

Ethnocultural Voices Series
Multicultural History Society of Ontario

Editorial Board

Paul Robert Magocsi, Editor in Chief

Yves Frenette   Roberto Perin
Wsevolod Isajiw   Lillian Petroff
Gabriele Scardellato   Harold Troper

Picture Brides

Japanese Women in Canada

Tomoko Makabe

Translated by Kathleen Chisato Merken

Multicultural History Society of Ontario

Picture Brides is based on a book published in Japanese by Mirai-sha, Tokyo in 1983.

Published with the assistance of the Ontario Ministry of Citizenship and the Ministry of Culture, Tourism and Recreation.

Canadian Cataloguing in Publication Data

Makabe, Tomoko, 1944–
   Picture brides: Japanese women in Canada

   (Ethnocultural voices)
   Includes bibliographic references.
   ISBN 0-919045-68-5

   1. Japanese – Canada – Biography. 2. Women immigrants – Canada – Biography. 3. Intercountry marriage – Canada – History. I. Multicultural History Society of Ontario. II. Title. III. Series.

   FC106.J3M3 1995   306.48'8951071   C95-932972-2
   F1035.J3M3 1995

© 1995 Multicultural History Society of Ontario
All rights reserved

No part of this publication may be reproduced, transmitted, or used in any form without written permission from the Multicultural History Society of Ontario.

Cover design by Tapanainen Graphics, Toronto
Printed and bound by the University of Toronto Press

***Picture Brides* is available from:**
   University of Toronto Press
   5201 Dufferin Street
   North York, Ontario, Canada M3H 5T8
   Order Fulfillment 1-800-565-9523

Contents

Preface		vii
Introduction		1
1	A Hundred Years of Japanese–Canadian History	17
2	Mrs Maki Fukushima	37
3	Mrs Hana Murata	67
4	Mrs Yasu Ishikawa	93
5	Mrs Tami Nakamura	127
6	Mrs Miyo Hayashi	151
Afterword		177
Further Reading		179

Preface

Since the second printing of the book in Tokyo in 1984, I have been asked repeatedly whether I would be translating it into English. The questioners assured me that the topic and contents would be of great interest to many audiences in Canada. Now I realize that over ten years have passed.

Fortunately, Kathleen Merken, from Montreal, discovered the book and took a personal interest in it. So much so that she volunteered to do the translation. Kathleen, with her academic background, not only in the Japanese language, but also in modern Japanese literature, is, I believe, the foremost English-Japanese translator in Canada and I was more than pleased with the final product.

Kathleen smoothed out the peculiar language and expressions used by the women, a dialect mixed with immigrant-invented Japanese–English, and with which I recall struggling when I was writing the book in Japanese.

In the meantime, I have had the opportunity of meeting many young Japanese Canadians across the country from the *Sansei* (third generation) and even the *Yonsei* (fourth generation). Through my research projects and personal contacts, I became acquainted with them personally. I noticed that these young members of our community have a strong sense of regret and sadness: because of the language barrier, they have been unable to relate to their grandparents and it was too late for many even to get to know them as persons.

These young people have assimilated "too well" and had lost the chance to hear the personal histories and experiences of their predecessors in this country. Almost all of the pre-war immigrant generation have passed away some years ago.

I hope this book will help narrow the gap a bit and, at the same time, deepen the understanding between the generations in our community. The stories of the *Issei* (first generation) women, described here as picture brides, have a great deal to interest readers and students, particularly in women's studies perhaps, including young Japanese–Canadian women. A Sansei women told me she would have asked, had there been no difficulty in communicating such very simple questions to her grandmother: "What happened in your life? Why did you come to Canada? What did you believe in, and dream of? Were you happily married?"

This English edition has an addition to the original book. In Chapter 1, on Japanese–Canadian history, there is a brief account of the Japanese–Canadian redress issue which took place in the 1980s.

We are indebted to Catherine A. Waite of the Multicultural History Society of Ontario for the editorial side of the book. The final manuscript has been significantly improved by her editing and suggestions.

Lastly, this book would not have been possible, of course, without the cooperation of the five women and the many other Issei women whom I have met. They always talked to me with such willingness and kindness, although a bit shyly. All of the five women in the book are gone now. Mrs Maki Fukushima, the last, died peacefully a few years ago after her 104th birthday. I still miss them very much.

Tomoko Makabe
Toronto, Canada
Summer 1995

Introduction

Meiji Women

I became interested in the history of immigrant women because I was an immigrant who made a firm resolve to live in a foreign society as a woman alone. I had come to Canada as a student, and by the time my studies were over, I felt that I wanted to establish myself in this society.

My field was sociology, with a special research interest in Canadian society. I wanted an actual experience of what I had studied for seven years. Having learned in detail about the experiences of the Japanese who had come before me, I had come to think that my role was to follow in their footsteps—to try to live and to work as an immigrant and as a member of the minority group of Japanese Canadians. My legal status as an immigrant, which I had assumed almost unwillingly during my student days, was a major factor in facilitating my decision. I was able to become a due and proper member of Canadian society at large.

With a population of approximately three million, Toronto, Ontario is the largest city in Canada and it has the greatest number of Japanese Canadians. At present, they are said to number from 25,000 to 30,000, including semi-permanent residents. During my many years as a student in Toronto, I had met many Japanese Canadians and became friendly with a number of them. I was fascinated by the stories told to me by the *Issei* (first-generation), the pioneers. Their tales about the old days, related in their old-fashioned, regional speech, were so interesting that I seized every chance to ask them to talk to me. When they heard I was from Japan, they seemed to grow nostalgic, and sometimes, a normally taciturn individual would become voluble.

The Issei have a chronic source of discontent: there is a practically, inpenetrable language barrier between them and their *Nisei* (second-generation) children that prevents them from holding real conversations. Some of the people were so happy to be able to talk at long last that we never ran out of topics, and I consciously strove to ask about everything in detail.

I had been in Canada for ten years, and had at last come to perceive my surroundings clearly, when I started to hear that old age was beginning to ravage the Issei, and I kept hearing about deaths among them. Nearly all the people who knew the pioneer days, those who had crossed the ocean near the turn of the century, had died. Even those in good health were in their eighties or nineties. An idea was ripening: I would ask a great many more people for their stories and put them in order. However, I kept procrastinating, and time passed.

In the late 1970s I chanced to make friends with some old Issei women in the neighbourhood who were also *Meiji* women (people in the Meiji period in Japan, 1868–1911). Most of these ladies were widows, bearing up under a solitary life, often proudly alone. They were reticent Japanese women. While their husbands had been alive, they behaved normally for women brought up in the Meiji period, an era of male privilege. They were unobtrusive, and say that they did not often speak with other people. Therefore they were unused to thinking about their experiences in any detail or putting them in order. When it came time for them to talk, each one made the same protest: "We don't know anything; all we've done is to live a long time." In general, they were modest and close-mouthed.

However, old age was steadily taking its toll on their memories. It made me impatient and anxious to think that if I missed this chance, I would never be able to listen to the women of this generation express their feelings and learn about their "lifetime full of hardships." Three years earlier, with the thought that it was urgent to make friends with many Issei, and form a pipeline to their memories, I began in earnest the preparations for an oral history of pioneering as told by immigrants.

Even though I had talked to a great number of people, I still felt I had not heard enough stories. Therefore I made every effort to attend Issei meetings and socials. There were picnics held by associations of people from the same region in Japan, which gave them a chance to socialize. As we ate together, I heard tales of enormous picnic feasts in the old days, and the amount of work that went into preparing the food.

Among the people living out their lives in old age homes, many had reached a very advanced age, but a good number were eager to tell their stories. Though they were all struggling with old age, they were in amazingly good health. When I visited their houses or apartments, they often regaled me with tea and sushi, while they talked on and on. At times, I was favoured by being invited to celebrations in hotels, and as I looked at the Issei in their places of honour, I would be treated to yet another feast. I believe I gained an insider's and an outsider's look at Issei life.

Now when I recall the ways of life of the Issei with whom I dealt, they are more or less similar to each other, and it is strange that none has left any extraordinary impression on me. I did not see any life which could be called luxurious, even to be complimentary, but neither did I encounter any extreme poverty.

No matter whose house I went to, the interiors were astonishingly similar, giving an impression of sheer simplicity and frugal habits. As a rule, the most expensive items of decoration were one or two uncommonly large Japanese dolls. On the wall would be hanging a rather cheap, Japanese landscape scroll, and, strewn around under it, items like Western dolls—a classic jumble of Japanese and Western objects. The covers on the tables and chairs had seen much use, and tended to be shabby and unfashionable. For some reason the décors were identical, and if there is such a thing as a common denominator among immigrants from all countries, this type of decor would exemplify it. The Issei, even if they have money, are said to lack any interest whatever in buying such things as expensive furniture. It may be that the thriftiness ingrained in these immigrants brought up in the Meiji period was accentuated by the habits of the impoverished life they had been used to before the war.

The same spirit of reserve appeared to pervade their eating habits. The special dishes cooked with care and consideration evoked the style of life of the Issei. Eels, even the canned sort, are a special treat. Apparently, a widow living alone finds it wasteful to eat a whole can by herself, even if it is a gift. Therefore, she will not open one unless she has a guest. In the hands of a woman like this, one tin of eels becomes a meal for two. With the addition of bits of *konnyaku* jelly and vegetables, the eels make a topping for bowls of rice. As I shared such meals, I remembered what a Nisei had told me: "The Issei can't ever let themselves spend." This same man said he enjoys taking his parents to restaurants now and then, but since they feel it is a waste of money, they probably take no pleasure in the meals.

While I helped the Issei women prepare these meals, and was treated to home-made noodles or rice cakes with sweet bean paste, I began to listen to the stories which emerged bit by bit. Though they tried to cut them short, saying that their talk about an ordinary woman's life had no value, I cajoled and encouraged them, and I listened closely, knowing that as they casually told their stories, I would be witnessing the history of a minority group in Canada.

The five Issei women who appear in this book are those, among the many of my acquaintance, whose stories I was able to hear in particular detail. I recorded them, as faithfully as possible, as they were told to me. I listened to the stories many times, even many dozens of times. Thinking it best to make a record of their speech because of the dialect words which were unfamiliar to me, and the special expressions used among the Issei, I began to insist on using a tape recorder. Thus I was able to preserve part of the interviews. The portions not recorded were supplemented by my memory and my notes. I was striving to gather life histories, one by one, so that I could collect them in a single history of immigrant women.

The personal life history of these five women, involving various degrees of good or bad fortune, is marked by nuances distinguishing her from the others, even when their experiences were similar. All five are over the age of 80, and have lived in Canada for more than 60 years. At present, they have settled in their respective regions, and are quietly living out their last years.

Only two of them live with their husbands, both of whom are more than 90 years old. They are spending the rest of their lives as couples caring for each other. These two women are living with a slowly growing sense of watching over husbands who will die in the near future. They live for nursing and housework, at the same time as they struggle with their own old age.

The other three women are widows. Apparently, 20 or 30 years of living alone means that individuality emerges and each, in her own way, has developed her own style and habits. They may have become accustomed to being alone and have developed the art of enjoying that life style, but they haven't been able to escape loneliness. Perhaps they fenced themselves off and avoided contact with outsiders. That feeling, I believe, appears naturally in the narration of their life histories. These are women who are facing the struggles of old age and ultimately death, alone.

When I recall the five protagonists, I am not struck by differences in personality, character or environment. Just as the interior decoration and everyday habits of these Issei are uniform, their character, habits, and attitudes to daily life are reflected in such amazing similarity that they have fused into one in my mind. Is it because more than 60 years of immigrant life in Canada have swallowed up subtle differences, and made these individuals—at a time when they are approaching the end of their lives—into one uniform type? Or is this another sign of homogeneity, that very particular Japanese trait?

All five women were "picture brides." There are differences among them depending on when they immigrated during the decade 1910–1920—the peak period for picture brides—or whether they married after one or two meetings with a man who had returned to Japan to take a wife or through an exchange of photos, without ever having met him.

All the women came to Canada as brides. They were approximately 20-years old and four were from rural or small-village families. They all "came without knowing anything at all." What could these inexperienced, young women have imagined their lives would be like "going to America," as the wives of immigrants?

I wanted to learn their true feelings. All five said that they had firmly decided that they must work, and that they wanted to work with all their might. With that spirited attitude, with intense emotion, and with a strong sense of adventure, they left their homes and came to Canada to live with men they did not know. To explain their emotions, all five use the word *akogare* (longing). They had a general expectation that marvellous things were in store for them. But they also had specific ambitions and motives: to succeed and make large sums of money by working. "I wanted to make so much money that I could set up a bank"; "I wanted to rebuild my parents' broken-down house."

The Japan of 70 years ago, from the Taisho to the Showa periods, saw a time of rapid industrial growth and urbanization. It was not impossible for young women to go to the big cities and find work, but those who could support themselves through their occupations were limited to the category of "progressive" women. It was almost impossible for a country-bred, uneducated, ordinary woman to become independent, either economically or socially. Going to Canada or the United States was practically the only means of improving one's status. Among the five Issei in this book, one is a graduate of the girls' high school system and one spent two years in a practical midwives' course in the supplementary education system. For women born in the 1890s, they were among the fortunate. It is said that Japanese women who immigrated to North America both before and after World War I were better educated than their contemporaries.

The subjects in this book were young women with a strong drive to work and to make money. They say they did not want to end up getting married in their villages, and that they had a vague desire to do something else. They also declared that if passage from Japan had been unrestricted, they might have crossed the ocean alone, not as brides. The strength of that desire could be felt, even in their casual conversations, and it made a strong impression on me.

From a modern perspective, the picture-bride system may seem too utilitarian and unnatural in its disregard of human qualities. It can also be seen as a last-resort measure born of necessity and of Asian pragmatism. From the brides' viewpoint, a typical attitude was "I would have married anybody, as long as I could get to America."

It was a once-in-a-lifetime gamble. But to the young women who jumped at this chance, the system was not so unnatural. They had won the approval of their parents, and they had the sober attitude that all they needed was a healthy man without eccentricities, so that they could probably manage to live with him. They do not remember closely scrutinizing the groom's character or prospects, such as his occupational background or future plans. The fact that they were picture brides also does not mean they married reluctantly. I did not find a single case of a bride who had been coaxed or urged by her parents and the people around her to cross the Pacific against her will. On the contrary, many women pushed aside their parents' and neighbours' disapproval and fears in order to embark on marriage.

Although these Issei women were not uneasy about the step they were taking, neither were they particularly expectant. They did not have any romantic fantasies. They say, from a distance of more than 60 years, that the only thing in their minds was a desire to go to America. Even though they spoke casually, as though discussing a third person, the listener could sense the sheer youthful eagerness of the migrant, without any dark undertones. Going to America was a great dream, a great longing. On this point, there was no difference between the men and women, or between the old-timer and the contemporary immigrant.

I was astonished and perplexed to hear that they felt no deep emotion at the idea of meeting and marrying an unknown man in a foreign land. But this lack of reaction is probably a result of the distance of time. The lapse of six decades is no doubt too long a time to have retained the feeling of a moment, even if that moment was a major event in a lifetime and no matter how dramatic the form it took. It was rare to hear one of these women reveal that she remembered being exceedingly bashful and embarrassed at the first meeting.

Among the many cases I studied, some women seem to have made their decisions in a state of impatience, thinking that if they missed this chance, they might never be able to cross the Pacific. Others made the decisions blindly. People familiar with the peak period for picture brides declare that a many of these women came knowing full well that their behaviour was irrational and unnatural. As a result, they had some trying experiences and both tragic and comic events took place. This premise is clear from the examples offered by two of the five brides in this volume.

We cannot, however, assert categorically that many failures and tragedies occurred because the system of arranged marriages, with all its unnaturalness and its uncertainties, was carried over to a foreign country. In Japan, too, many marriages of the day were irrational; they were made solely for practical reasons. Women made alliances despite a lack of affection, some were plagued by continuous bad luck, and others entered catastrophic marriages merely for the sake of appearances. These are phenomena not only of the past, but also of the present and occurred everywhere in Japan and throughout the world.

Finally, the long-dreamed-of passage to America was realized, although the country, against all expectations, turned out to be

Canada. The life of an immigrant was waiting for the picture brides as soon as they arrived. Before World War I, the great majority of immigrants were labourers and everyone worked, both men and women. In no case was a bride destined to be simply a housewife caring for her own family. Early in a marriage, these women might go into the mountains, work in the fields or on the fishing grounds, or in other people's houses as maids (then known as doing "housework"). Most continued to do such work for decades. From the beginning, the brides were confronted by a struggle between labour and life.

As they worked, these Issei women gave birth and raised many children and maintained households. They never made a sharp distinction between work and family, and never had any problem as to which was more important. Neither aspect could be singled out for exclusive attention, since they had been linked from the very beginning. Many Japanese Canadians were farmers, and the women's work was not limited to supplementary or temporary contributions. It is accurate to say that they participated equally with their husbands in the production process. The same relationship was found in the fishing industry; the wives worked practically on the same level as their husbands.

The early immigrant woman's work deserves special mention because she played much more than a simple, supplementary role. Women worked uncultivated lands and the forests, joined in the clearing of the wilderness, and engaged directly in agricultural production. Not until 50 years later did Canadian society properly acknowledge the backbreaking labour of the Japanese–Canadian pioneers in developing the agriculture, fishing and forestry industries which are so basic to the country's economy. Half of the pioneers were women, and the intensity of their struggle was in no way inferior to that of the men.

Before the war, most immigrants were uniformly poor, no matter where one looked. The life of immigrants from East Asia was particularly hard. None of them came with money or property. Without the money they saved from their labours, they could not own land or houses. Therefore, competition was unavoidable.

These old-timers say they worked hard because they thought they had to do as well as the other Japanese immigrants. The Issei had an extraordinary capacity for work; their Nisei children attest to this trait unanimously and with great admiration. One sentence, simple but full of emotion, conveys the struggles of these five women: all of them say, "I think I really worked very hard." This statement involves a complicated mixture of feelings: nostalgia for youth, a wistful attachment to memories of toiling away in silence, and also a slight sense of emptiness, as if everything had been useless. Finally, a trace of pride underlies their words, "It's amazing that I came through it all right," as if they cannot help wondering how they did.

No matter how severe the struggle, once it is over, it becomes "just an ordinary thing to do." This statement implies that most Japanese Canadians were poor and that life was very difficult. Some of them even explain that suffering could be borne more easily because it was a shared experience. When the Issei talk about the old days, saying "We weren't the only poor people. Everybody around us was the same," they are explaining things away: if everyone was the same, then their experiences were ordinary. This is necessarily an affirmation of both the past and of reality as "ordinary."

When the Issei speak of "everybody around us," they mean Japanese immigrants. The people generally called "whites" included many immigrants like them, but non-Japanese did not fit into their general scheme of things. The Issei's frame of reference is limited to "Japanese–Canadian society."

From the very first stages of settlement in Canada, Japanese Canadians became used to living together in one location. Wherever they went they constructed a small, Japanese-only society called Little Tokyo, in a sort of "settlement" and lived huddled together within it. During World War II, internment-camp life was forced upon them, but once there, the Issei returned, in effect, to their Japanese villages, and lived there for several years.

Most of the people, for their entire life, were unable to abandon their settlements and to see themselves as part of the greater society.

It was natural for the Issei to cluster together, because they had been excluded and discriminated against from their first encounters with Canada and, on top of that, they declared they did not know a word of English. The minds of the Issei constructed a Japanese settlement, and the effect was far more than physical. In the 30 and more years after World War II, they lived scattered throughout the country. Although the old settlements had vanished completely, the psychological ones remained. The Issei lived dispersed across the country, but they did not enter Canadian society. When Canada finally opened its doors to accept Japanese Canadians formally as members of society, the process of socialization among the Issei was already completed. The Issei had thoroughly adapted to Japanese–Canadian society, which resembled a neighbourhood association, with its spirit of mutual aid and its sharing of the ups and downs of life. It can also be said that they were too old to enter society at large and to adapt to it when the time finally came to do so, after the war. Thus for the Issei, Canada was to the very end a foreign society that had little relation to them. It was not their own society and it was not suited to their nature.

As far as the Issei were concerned, the standard of judgment in all matters was limited to Japanese Canadians and their society. This mentality was probably stronger among the women than the men. As the women admitted, "We've been living here not knowing anything, even after sixty years, and we don't even know English." For Issei women, contact with the outside world was perhaps limited. Even those who worked on the same level as men, or ran businesses with an exclusively white clientele, had a generally narrow social view, and their lives were extremely circumscribed. What amazed me the most about these women was the narrowness of that social view. The clearest example can be seen in the problems of exclusion and discrimination.

In discussions about the past with Japanese Canadians, the subjects that inevitably arise are exclusion and discrimination. It is impossible to relate Japanese–Canadian history without considering the viciousness of society's attitudes towards East Asians in general. It is also impossible to understand present-day Japanese–Canadian society outside that context. The Issei discuss the subject with passion, sometimes in tones full of anger. There is no end to the specific examples of discrimination they experienced in daily life.

After World War II, the social climate in Canada changed completely, and exclusion disappeared with incredible speed. How could such things have happened in the past? The passing years have provided enough time to marvel at it. Some people even say that since times have changed for the better, the past should be forgotten. However, as far as I know, it is only the men who continue to say that they can never forget, even if they should try to do so.

In British Columbia, where more than 90 per cent of the Japanese Canadians lived before World War II, the situation was so extreme that not a day passed without anti-Japanese attitudes being voiced. Over and over again, prejudice would break out with a vengeance, in every form possible. A global view of the history of exclusion of East Asians in Canada shows clearly that racism was extremely deep-rooted. It was a product of colonialism which held sway throughout the world for a long time, and which the British Empire brought to its colony, Canada. The notion of Anglo-Saxon racial superiority took hold of the minds of the timid, white colonials and remained. From today's perspective, it can be seen as morbid.

For Japanese Canadians, the workplace was the stage on which they competed with white labourers inculcated with racism. In the labour unions, the various racial groups vied with each other ever more bitterly, clashing in the struggle for jobs. In the half-century, or between their first encounter with the whites and the beginning of the World War II, the Japanese Canadians consistently had to submit to low wages in their struggle for existence. And, working for low wages turned out to be in itself a cause of various types of discrimination. Among the Issei, the mechanisms of the situation were fully understood only by the men, who felt resentment, and who carried that feeling to the end of their lives. Very rarely did the women react in the same way. This fact was a source of wonder to me.

My talks with the women revealed at once that they were less accustomed than the men to discrimination as a personal experience. It is extremely curious that for the women, who saved up a certain amount of their wages as domestic workers, or who engaged in business as dressmakers, the consciousness of being forced to work for low pay and the sense of severe competition with whites were so slight as to be practically nonexistent. The women are unanimous in saying that they have no memory of having asked how much lower wages were for Asians than for whites, even though they were doing the same work. Yet it is a fact that wages were commonly 30 per cent lower. Neither do the Issei women show any sign of having been suspicious, since they thought from the beginning that wages differed according to race. The women cover this point, too, saying that it could not be helped, as they themselves were not singled out for exploitation; all of "the people around me" were subject to the same kind of treatment.

The women also regarded people as individuals and not part of a group. For example, they said that white people were all very well-intentioned, as employers, co-workers, and occasionally as neighbours. But how can they close their eyes to certain facts: that white people, individually kind and well-intentioned, gathered together to set up a large number of anti-Asian groups, and that the power of those organizations carried out extremely anti-Japanese activities, over and over again? How can they be so willing to overlook other facts: that the government, made up of "really kind white people, if you took them one by one," robbed them of their right to vote, excluded the Japanese by all means possible, and tried to drive them out of the country, sending them "back" to Japan?

Certainly, the Issei are people of the Meiji era. Since the education of women was directed entirely towards caring for the household, the statement "I came without knowing anything" perhaps expresses fidelity to that ideal, rather than self-deprecation. It is a cruel fact that the enthusiasm of the young brides who crossed the ocean with the ambition of becoming rich dissolved in the blink of an eye, even before their struggle with a harsh existence. Perhaps we should regard them as individuals who did their utmost in life: they focused primarily on survival as members of a minority group, within a climate of prejudice and discrimination, and they bore a number of children to raise within both Japanese and Canadian culture. Perhaps, too, hard realities forced an attitude of compromise, so that they warded off misfortune by "thinking it was naturally like that": a technique for ensuring their own survival.

The Japanese–Canadian society in which the Issei lived was a small and narrow one. They shut themselves up in it, resulting, if we look critically at Canadian society as a whole, in the fact that they were completely unable to regard their own situation objectively. They closed their eyes to injustice and wrongs, saying "it can't be helped," and not once did they stir up their anger to reveal it to the outside world. It appears that Meiji-born women in particular were fated never to open their eyes to society.

The history of immigrants, whether Japanese or not, has been almost exclusively the history of male immigrants. Almost all the characters are men; only the lives of men are reported; and events are interpreted by these men and become historical facts. The Japanese women who appear in recent immigrant history have been limited to the so-called *karayuki-san*, those who went southward in Asia for specific work purposes "as women." The period when Japanese women called *karayuki-san* (literally, women going oversees) crossed the ocean, and the history of their lives as producers, should be considered a noteworthy process in modernization. But why should the study of women by sociologists and historians be limited to a single group, such as the karayuki-san? Women do not appear in orthodox histories. The history of Japanese immigrants to North America does not differ on this point. To the present, only the history where men are the heroes has been told.

The Japanese made many painful contributions as they engaged in opening up the forestry, fishing, and agriculture industries in British Columbia in the early stage of development. Soon after the turn of the century, as a result of anti-Japanese activity, the number of immigrants permitted to enter the country was severely limited, and constituted a very slight percentage of the total number of people allowed into the country.

Considering the severe exclusion and discrimination against their small numbers, Japanese Canadians have contributed more than their share to the country's history. Surely, if immigration had been unrestricted, if the Japanese had been allowed to enter the country as freely as immigrants from elsewhere, the development of Western Canada would have taken another direction particularly in the area of agriculture, where they had demonstrated their superior abilities. The Issei, if they had been given full scope to develop, would have changed enough of the agricultural basics as to alter how this industry developed in Canada. The results could have been revolutionary, such as those produced by Japanese immigrants in Brazil.

While giving full rein to such thoughts, I do not wish to forget the pioneer wives. They must not be forgotten. These women joined their men in order to go into wild, uncleared territories to work 15 hours a day, and who declare that they can be proud of that, at least. Most of them have already died, disregarded and absent from written records. Should they be left forgotten forever? These are women who have never been on centre stage, they are wives and mothers who have lived in silence without even being aware of the role they were playing. It is my wish to give these women a hearing, however modest in scope, before they all disappear from our view.

Research into women's history has just begun. If it progresses and historians—men included—come forth to undertake histories involving women, methods of historiography will change, and a broader field of knowledge will develop. I have recorded the stories of five Japanese women who live in Canada and who talked to me. Their stories have been set down just as they told them, but their names have all been altered, because of their unanimous request.

1 A Hundred Years of Japanese–Canadian History

According to the records, the first Japanese person to reside in Canada was a man named Manzo Nagano from the Nagasaki Prefecture who came in 1877. One hundred years later, in 1977, Canadians of Japanese origin observed his arrival with major celebrations called "the Year of the Japanese–Canadian Centennial." The Nisei and *Sansei* (third generation), who planned the festivities called for the general public throughout Canada to participate. Thus a year that commemorated Japanese–Canadian history broke out of the limits of the community and developed into a national festival, showing the evolution of this group over a period of 100 years.

Today, persons of Japanese descent in Canada, including temporary residents connected with Japan-based companies, number approximately 60,000. With a total population 27 million people in Canada, the number of people with Japanese origin is especially low, even among the many ethnic groups which make up this small country. Constituting barely 0.2 per cent, it is truly a minority group.

Before World War II, 90 per cent of all Japanese Canadians lived on the West Coast, in British Columbia. After the war they dispersed throughout Canada. The war broke up the community which had been scattered and isolated and, accordingly its members, it underwent a rebirth. The account below traces the course of Japanese–Canadian history during the century.

Japanese immigration to Canada began in earnest after the turn of the 20th century. Manzo Nagano's presence, and that of a few others, were exceptions. The main migration began approximately 20 years after the start of the main thrust of immigration to North America, in particular to Hawaii and the United States mainland. Only part of the stream was directed to Canada.

From early times, people came and went without settling in the country for such purposes as fishing. The national census of 1901 counted fewer than 5,000 persons of Japanese ancestry. In 1911, the figure had increased to 9,000. But it was still insignificant compared to the several million immigrants who had come to Canada at the time. It is safe to say that all the Japanese immigrants in the early period were unmarried men seeking temporary work. Many of them drifted on to the United States or they were seasonal labourers who returned to Japan after the end of the fishing season. The same was true of the rest: most were classic immigrants of the migrant-worker type, who planned to save their money for several years and then return home.

After the Russo-Japanese War ended in 1905, immigration to Canada enjoyed a vogue in Japan, but entry restrictions were already in place. The Canadian government had negotiated with the Japanese government to limit voluntarily its number of emigrants. The sentiment for the exclusion of Asian immigrants was growing stronger every day in British Columbia, and a continued, unrestricted entry of Japanese immigrants would damage the interests of both Canada and Japan. The results of the negotiations were announced in 1908 as the Gentlemen's Agreement, or the Lemieux Agreement. It limited the annual number of immigrants to 400. The agreement was amended twice, in 1924 and 1928, but each time it retained limitations on the number of immigrants and the categories of their occupations.

Why did the Japanese settle only in British Columbia, where exclusion was so harsh? Why didn't they move somewhere else? British Columbia was the shortest distance from Japan, just on the other side of the Pacific Ocean, and that's where the immigrants disembarked. If they had moved to the interior, they would have been faced with transportation and other expenses. As well, the geography and climate of this province resembled Japan most closely, and even the winters were mild and easy to endure. The Issei settled in the Vancouver area because of its strong appeal, surrounded as it was by mountains and the sea. At the turn of the century, the Canadian West was in the process of development.

It was also relatively easy, even for newcomers, to gain employment in the province's basic industries of fishing, forestry, and mining. The stories about men finding work the day they arrived were no exaggeration. As for the type of work, there was nothing but simple labour and wages were minimal. Even so, they amounted to several times more than that the men would have received in Japan as farmers or craftsmen. Therefore they worked with the sole thought of saving their money and returning home.

Many Japanese men engaged in fishing and forestry, in the latter case both as tree fellers and sawmill hands. Not only did they lack the technical knowledge and capital to secure better positions; they did not know English, the essential and official language. They usually worked for a Japanese subcontractor in all-Japanese groups which were generally composed of men from the same prefecture or region in Japan.

Once they had accumulated experience and earned some capital, the way to success was through self-employment and independent enterprise. They aimed at economic advancement by obtaining land and farming it, by buying fishing gear and becoming independent fishermen, or by entering some form of commercial activity in the cities. Since the 1920s were the years when the Issei finally reached temporary economic stability and consolidated their position, such as it was, about 20 years had passed since they had begun to arrive. By this time, they had also come to understand that their dream of saving money and returning to Japan was utterly out of the question.

Once their lives had stabilized and they had found their feet to some extent, they started wanting families. Those already married sent for the wives and children they had left behind, and established households. Among the bachelors, some went back to Japan to get married and others married through exchanges of photographs and first met their brides in Canada. The peak period for Issei marriages, and the formation of their families, was from the end of the 1910s through the 1920s. All five of the women who appear in this book came to Canada as brides during this period.

Almost all the Japanese women who entered the country in these years came as brides to men who had already established themselves. Also awaiting them was a society of Japanese Canadians, already in place. Although the foundation had been laid, the history of these five women make it clear how impoverished that life was to be and how harsh the labours.

Underlying the reminiscences of these brides of yesteryear, who are unanimous in saying "it was a rougher life than it was in Japan," is a reflection of the hardships the men endured under the most adverse conditions. The men, lacking any amusements or culture, spent their lives on the mountains or on the fishing grounds, with only their fellow Japanese immigrants to rely upon. Such was the world these women entered.

Around 1941, when the Pacific war began, the Japanese-Canadian population was more than 23,000, and a number of organizations in each community in the various regions had already been formed and firmly consolidated. It was the period when the Nisei generation, born and educated in Canada, was growing up and about to strike out on its own. The Issei had emerged from the position of lowest unskilled labourers, and had been recognized as workers seriously striving to raise their standard of living. Since they worked well, and for low wages, they were valuable to employers. However, no matter what their occupation, the wages of Asian workers were about 30 per cent lower than those of whites. Since the differential wage rate was institutionalized, the Issei were resigned to it. One indication of the Issei's progress is that they were engaged in 60 occupations.

In particular, Japanese Canadians excelled in fishing and farming, and they were regarded as very strong competitors to white workers.

Fishing was the industry where the Japanese made the speediest progress. They engaged in salmon fishing on the principal fishing grounds of the Fraser River, with activities centred on the fishing village of Steveston. When the season came, several thousand Japanese–Canadian fishermen might go out to work: they were even said to dominate fishing in British Columbia. Fishing, the industry with the fiercest competition among the races, was also the field where anti-Japanese feeling was the strongest. Japanese-Canadian farming families had succeeded, though on a small scale, along the Fraser and in the interior, in growing vegetables and fruit, especially strawberries, and gave promise of improving further.

Inevitably, newcomers to any country face a difficult path. Every immigrant struggles, hoping for success, and competition is unavoidable. The Issei, who worked for long hours for low wages, were criticized for being content with a low standard of living, and became fearsome competitors versus white labourers for jobs. That was a reason for exclusion and discrimination. When they were excluded, and their places of work restricted, the struggle for existence became all the more acute. They had to work harder than ever they had in the past. The Issei repeated this process for 40 years in Canada, till the war began. Considering the conditions imposed on the Japanese around that time, the work the Issei accomplished on the west coast of Canada was immense.

Racial prejudice among the people of British Columbia before the war continues to be a topic for discussion. Some historians consider racism as a phenomenon of abnormal psychology, and attempt to explain its roots through social psychology. In a recently established, immigrant society with shallow roots—nearly half of the people in the province were immigrants—all strove for success. In a society composed solely of timid and ignorant workers, prejudice was like an attack of fever. Some sociologists explain that economic competition and struggles for position among ethnic groups led to the original confrontations, in which the powerful tried to drive out the weak.

The whites, many of British stock, were firmly convinced that Canada should be a white people's country. They genuinely feared that British Columbia would be slowly eroded by coloured races from Asia. The Yellow Peril theory, which was in fact completely unfounded, reigned supreme.

It was considered absolutely impossible for people of Asian origin, because they were too different from whites in race, language, religion and customs, to assimilate and "become like whites." The whites, not satisfied merely with limiting the entry of immigrants, believed that the only solution was to send them back to their lands of origin. After all, the Asians already present could not be eliminated only by limiting immigration. In prewar British Columbia, many groups were organized for the sole purpose of excluding Asians. The labour unions, too, preached and practised exclusion. Not one of their leaders attempted to admit Asians to their unions. There was not one case of workers transcending race and uniting to, for example, take strike action.

A 1907 demonstration of the Asiatic Exclusion League, which had been formed in Vancouver, turned into a riot, and the Chinese and Japanese neighbourhoods saw scenes of violence. As a result of this riot, the federal government reinforced its limitation on immigrants.

The most effective measures used in British Columbia to exclude Asian Canadians were public pressures through laws and ordinances. The Gentlemen's Agreement between Canada and Japan had a great effect on limiting the numbers of Japanese immigrants. During the 1930s, the number of Japanese entering the country was drastically reduced, to the point that it almost ceased. The same type of restriction, although harsher, had been applied to Chinese immigrants from an even earlier date. At the time of entry, the Chinese were subject to a head tax, which in

1904 was raised to 500 dollars, a considerable amount, even in our day. If they could pay this sum, Chinese people could enter the country. However, in 1923, the federal government passed the Chinese Exclusion Act, which finally put an end to Chinese immigrants. This was a political measure adopted under pressure from British Columbia.

At any rate, British Columbia was a place where the exclusion of Asians began soon after it became a province in 1871. In 1902 the legislature passed a law denying the franchise to Canadians of Asian origin, both native-born and naturalized, although all were nominally Canadian citizens. This law remained in effect for nearly 50 years: until 1947 for Canadians of Chinese and East Indian descent and 1949 for Japanese Canadians.

Denial of the franchise meant these individuals were unable to cast ballots because their names did not appear on the voters' rolls. It also involved practical disabilities of a more serious nature. Asian Canadians were deprived of the right to engage in certain professions, to obtain licences to start businesses, and to work for the government; in other words, they were robbed of their civil rights. They found themselves excluded from key fields of gainful employment and prevented from making economic progress.

The Nisei who were born in Canada were classified as Asian by race, and like the Issei, were denied the franchise. They referred to themselves cynically as "second class citizens." On graduating from university, no matter how well qualified they might be, the fields open to them were extremely limited. Not only were they barred from certain professions, but they could not even apply to teach in public schools. For the Nisei who came of age on the West Coast before the war, the weight of anti-Japanese feeling was a bitter fact of daily life. When they graduated from school and tried to find work, their eyes were finally and fatally opened to the realities of exclusion. Since Asians did not even have the right to cast a ballot, they lacked any political power. They were unable to raise a finger against the anti-Japanese laws and regulations which passed through the legislature one after the other.

To confront the anti-Japanese storm, the Issei retreated to their own community. Unable to survive without reliance on their fellows, they naturally lived together in clusters. It was said that wherever they lived, the Japanese had the habit of huddling together, but this tendency was not limited to the Japanese. Almost all ethnic groups have the same characteristic: in order to survive as minorities in a foreign society, they require solidarity, and thus, organizations for mutual assistance are formed. In the case of Asians, who were distinguished from whites by skin colour and their way of life, the degree of concentration was all the more noticeable. In turn, it became another reason for the majority to hate the Japanese. For Japanese Canadians, a community like Little Tokyo in Vancouver was a necessity. In their view, it provided a safety zone against the hostility of the society around them.

Since the streets of the Japanese district were lined with all manner of stores and organizations, business could generally be transacted without the use of English. To some extent, daily life could be carried on without reference to the outside society. The result was to push Japanese Canadians increasingly into separation and isolation, which in turn became a major obstacle to the assimilation of the Issei into Canadian society. The anti-Japanese movement argued that Japanese Canadians, as a group, never tried to assimilate. On the other hand, many Issei found comfort even in the slum-like Japanese district, because of its warm sense of communality.

A knowledge of the background behind the long-standing and deep-rooted feeling against the Japanese in British Columbia makes the war-time chain of events comprehensible. When the Pacific War broke out, Japanese Canadians were once again subjected to harsh treatment. Using the war as a pretext, the British Columbia government, thinking that Japanese Canadians could now be expelled from the province, moved into action. Because

Canada and Japan were at war, Japanese Canadians were regarded as enemy aliens. Two groups, the Canadian-born and the naturalized Issei, constituted over half the Japanese-Canadian population. However, they were regarded in the same light as those holding Japanese citizenship—as enemy aliens. The people were thus defined and categorized by racial origin alone.

It becomes even more apparent when one considers that Germany and Italy were also at war with Canada. However, there were millions of Canadians of German or Italian origin who were not regarded as enemy aliens. Therefore it is obvious that racial prejudice was deeply ingrained, and it dominated the politics and public opinion of the day. Only the Japanese–Canadian segment of the population was considered to be composed entirely of aliens. The federal government insisted that for reasons of national defense, they could not be allowed to continue living on the West Coast. There followed a series of "measures against enemy aliens" conducted by federal authorities.

The Canadian policy was set up in concert with that of the government of the United States. Japanese Canadians were subjected to the War Measures Act, and were deprived of all their civil rights. The government then determined to expel them from the Pacific coast and to relocate them 100 miles inland.

From early 1942, and continuing through that year, the government uprooted and expelled more than 20,000 Japanese Canadians from the West Coast area. Able-bodied adult males were placed in road camps to work on highway construction, and family units were sent to grow sugar beets in Alberta and Manitoba. In several different locations in the interior of British Columbia, temporary lodgings were hastily constructed to make internment camps. All the camps were in isolated, ruined locations known as "ghost towns."

In the camps, the inmates, primarily women and children, spent the war years in inactivity. In these so-called "safe cells," "our existence and our livelihood were protected," to quote one Issei. The Japanese Canadians who moved, left their homes believing it was a temporary evacuation for the sake of safety. They abandoned their property behind them which was all confiscated by the government. The farmlands, the fishing boats, the houses, the shops—all the property that the Issei had worked for so diligently, was sold for next to nothing. Therefore, the Japanese Canadians lost their economic base at the same time as the Pacific War started. From December 1941 to the summer of 1946, when resettlement was almost complete, they were considered as enemy aliens and deprived of their liberty. When freedom was finally returned, they had been stripped of everything. They were faced with starting all over again.

When the war ended, the Canadian government clarified its policy towards Japanese Canadians in the postwar period. The aim was to resolve the Japanese problem in British Columbia once and for all, and again, the attitude of the government was harsher than necessary with no observable leniency. Compared to the government of the United States, which had been moved to soften its approach by the loyal and heroic actions of Nisei soldiers on the battlefields of Europe, the Canadian authorities were, on the whole, high-handed and their policy lacked fairness.

The government did not immediately permit Japanese Canadians to return to their homes on the west coast. It wanted to prevent the Japanese–Canadian population from concentrating and forming colonies again. In fact, for four years after the end of the war, Japanese Canadians were not allowed to return to the coast. Those who wished to remain in Canada had to promise to move east of the Rockies and to live there, scattered. This was called the Dispersal Policy for the Japanese–Canadian population, who were strongly affected by it. This voluntary, yet forcible, dispersal was regarded as a test of loyalty to Canada.

Those individuals who hesitated to go to the unknown regions east of the Rockies were actively urged by the government to return to Japan. Arrangements were made so they could return voluntarily. For example, travel expenses for adults and children were paid by the government. These actions were inducements for

Japanese Canadians to go to Japan, rather than remain in Canada. The government's encouragement of repatriation was a success. For a time, nearly 10,000 Japanese signed applications to go to Japan. However, many applications were withdrawn when Japan's defeat had become a certainty and the actual number was around 4,000. Among the 4,000 were many children below the age of sixteen who were accompanying their parents. Many of the returnees had difficult experiences in settling in Japan immediately after the war.

Japanese Canadians above the age of sixteen were therefore faced with a choice: should they remain in Canada, scattered in the eastern provinces, or should they go to Japan? For some Nisei and Issei, the decision was made partly by their children who wanted to move east. Some changed their minds, and returned to Japan full of loathing for Canada. The anxieties of this period remained as deeply harboured, ill feelings.

Inwardly, the people felt resentment and anger at the government's query as to whether they wished to remain in their own country, the land of their birth. Clearly, they had not the slightest desire to "return" to Japan, which to them was a foreign country. But Canada also did not say that they would be accepted unconditionally as Canadians. They were obliged to follow the government policy of population dispersal, in order to demonstrate their loyalty to the country.

The war forced the Nisei to examine their identity as Canadians. Not for a moment could they think of themselves as Japanese, but on the other hand, they had not become totally Canadian. Even if they considered themselves exclusively Canadian, the society around them did not treat them as such. The Nisei suffered; they were left with deep psychological scars. At this point, their state of mind is a clue to understanding Nisei identity, and its changing patterns with the passing of time after resettlement.

In 1949, the franchise was granted to all Canadian citizens of Asian origin. At long last, Japanese Canadians became Canadians in fact as well as in name. The following year, the right to move back to British Columbia was granted, and among others, those wishing to enter the fishing industry gradually began to make their way back. But many people still say they never wish to set foot in British Columbia again. Those advocating resettlement in the east established themselves in various localities and tried for a new beginning. The big cities, especially Toronto, became the centres of resettlement, and even now the majority of Japanese Canadians live in the metropolitan area. A number of new immigrants and travellers settled in Vancouver and now, combined with those who returned after the war, the population of persons of Japanese descent is more than 10,000.

Japanese Canadians, no matter in what city they live, have been extremely careful to avoid living close to each other in colonies. They cooperated with the government which decreed that dispersion was the path to assimilation into Canadian society.

In the post-war recovery boom in Canada, the period from the 1950s to the 1960s, there was a great surge in economic growth. Under these favourable conditions, possibilities for work increased, and Japanese Canadians found it relatively easy to make a new start in life. Mixing with the great numbers of immigrants from many European countries, they progressed in their own fields. At first, even in big cities like Toronto, they were surrounded by people who had never seen a Japanese, so that they met discrimination from time to time, but racial prejudice of the kind they had known in British Columbia had vanished with incredible speed.

The open, energetic atmosphere of Eastern Canada appealed to the Japanese Canadians. They were seized by a desire to succeed and to prove themselves. Because of their diligence and honesty in work, and their eagerness to learn which earned them good results, they were recognized in no time at all by white employers. One by one, they gained the confidence of others, and when Japanese Canadians came to be recognized as trustworthy, the tempo of their economic and social ascent quickened.

After the war, many of the young Nisei found the path to university open to them and entered the professions. The economic advances made by this group were especially conspicuous. Such was the fruit borne of the efforts of the Japanese Canadians, with their intense respect for education, and particularly of the sacrifices made by the Issei. Most of them say all their efforts in the 30 plus years after the new beginning were validated by the advancements made by their offspring. Socially, the Japanese Canadians, especially the Nisei, rank themselves as middle-class. This pattern of social ascent is the same for those who made their new beginnings after their uprooting in Manitoba, Alberta, and elsewhere.

The *Sansei* are the postwar generation. Having grown up after the dispersal of the population, even the concept of a Japanese–Canadian community is somewhat alien to them. For them, racial prejudice and their families' forced removal are historical facts belonging to a distant past. An overwhelming number of Sansei proceed to university, and make their way in society, freely choosing their own paths. Since they feel no psychological tension as members of a minority group, they are the same as other Canadians in attitudes and in behaviour. The Sansei are the first generation to be completely Canadian, and at present, they constitute the majority of the Japanese–Canadian population.

Finally, a word about the new immigrants. In the 1950s, immigration from Japan resumed, but did not become substantial until the present. For a time, people continued to enter the country, sent for by relatives, but their numbers were insignificant. According to the government's immigration statistics, some 10,000 Japanese entered Canada between 1950 and 1980, for an annual average of about 300 individuals. Among this number, it appears there were many former repatriates who had returned to Japan after some years in Canada. From the 1960s, the number of immigrants from Asian countries such as Hong Kong, India and Pakistan increased sharply, in such numbers as to make the Japanese total negligible. In contrast to the Japanese experience, these immigrants unfailingly settled down just after entering Canada, and their numbers increased steadily.

In 1967 the immigration law was amended, and entry standards were greatly liberalized. Conditions became relatively easy for immigrants with the proper qualifications. They did not even need the help of liberalized laws, because this was a period of great economic growth in Japan. Many of the recent immigrants are people such as technicians, who reside in big cities. Like their predecessors, they are scattered over the entire territory of Canada, and are assimilating into society at large. They differ from the earlier immigrants both in their upbringing and in their motives for leaving Japan, and many of them live independently, with no attempt to depend on their precursors. Contact between the old and the new groups is limited to a small number of individuals.

Epilogue to Japanese–Canadian History: Redress

September 22, 1988, was an historic date for the Japanese–Canadian community and for Canada itself. That was the day when the Japanese–Canadian Redress Settlement was signed with the federal government, with unanimous support from all political parties. The announcement of this event came as a major surprise, as there had been no hint of the government presenting a bill which was acceptable to the Japanese–Canadian community.

The Canadian government formally acknowledged its errors in its policies and actions during and after World War II when it treated Canadians of Japanese ancestry as enemy aliens, regardless of citizenship. In addition, recognizing the injustice of their forced removal and internment, and of the resulting losses they suffered, the government awarded a token compensation in the amount of $21,000 to each surviving victim. Moreover, in recognition of the prewar Japanese–Canadian community which had been completely destroyed by the policy of forced dispersal, the government established a fund of $12,000,000 as compensation for the losses, and for rebuilding the community. The government's expenditures for the settlement amounted to about $40,000,000. It cost the government dearly to make this apology for the wrongdoings of a previous administration. The sum of $400,000,000 is equivalent to the amount required by an automobile manufacturer coming from overseas to set up a new assembly plant in Canada.

Six months after the Redress Settlement was negotiated, it was announced that the number of people who were both survivors as of 1988, and who had applied for individual compensation[1], exceeded the original estimate; there were some 15,000. There were also individuals who had left Canada under the repatriation program and now resided in Japan or elsewhere. It was necessary to contact all those who should be informed of the settlement. Both the government and the National Association of Japanese Canadians, which had carried on the redress movement, were aware that it would take five years of persevering work to complete the process.

The year 1977 marked the centennial of the start of immigration from Japan to Canada. And it was about this time that a few Japanese Canadians began to declare that they would like to take some action about the "disgraceful wartime events" which remained unresolved. In Toronto, in the province where Japanese Canadians resettled in the greatest numbers after the war, a group of about 100 volunteers began discussions. The group was formally organized in 1982, and another group formed in Vancouver around that time.

---

[1] Individual survivors eligible for compensation were Japanese Canadians born before March 1949, including those born during internment; these were persons permanently residing in Canada at the time of the order for the mass uprooting in 1942. Also eligible were Japanese Canadians who lived in provinces and territories other than British Columbia during the same period.

None the less, those who were ready to join the movement constituted a very small group. After the war, Japanese Canadians had done their utmost to work seriously and achieve economic stability, intent on rising above their former second-class status and be recognized as full members of society. They devoted all their energies to these goals. Thus, they had nothing left over for political activity, either materially or psychologically. Most of the Nisei who had been raised in British Columbia before the war still bore traces of the discrimination they had experienced, like deep scars. They had an ingrained belief that the best way to act was to avoid attracting attention to themselves—to avoid causing a stir in society.

There were also profound differences in attitudes among the Japanese–Canadian population, depending on the generation. Of the Issei born in the Meiji era, only a few hundred were still alive. Their true feelings may be summarized as: "I don't care any more. It's a bother just to collect my thoughts." At a time when so many members of their generation were dead, they felt it unfair to accept money as redress, just because they happened to have survived. Some were uneasy on this point.

Others members of the community even opposed the idea of financial compensation. Since "you can't put a price on suffering," money cannot restore anything. It made no sense to calculate the losses suffered at this late date, and at any rate, the individual differences among those who had or did not have property were so vast that the cases could not all be treated on the same level. As a result, most of the Issei appeared to think that any amount they received would do; it would be just for the sake of form, as part of the group called "Japanese Canadians."

The Issei were the most important among those eligible for compensation, but those who challenged the government and assumed the task of negotiation came from the post-war group, many of them Sansei. People who were not yet born at the time when these events took place were heading the movement. It would have been pointless to expect this generation to understand the complex ideas and expectations of their grandparents. It is safe to say that from beginning, no dialogue took place between these two generations. They had absolutely no basis for communication when it came to basic concepts such as human rights, freedom, or financial redress. The two groups lived in utterly different value systems.

Naturally, the redress movement did not develop without hitches. Initially, few supporters came forward. Furthermore, the community had no unified perspective and no coordination of purpose. The movement continued for five years and the very fact that it continued meant a series of difficulties. Since the events of 50 years ago were being brought up again, an infinite range of ideas, expectations and emotions emerged, so that problems inevitably became complicated. Agreement and consensus would have been unimaginable. Joy Kogawa, a Nisei writer, relates the process painstakingly in her recent novel *Itsuka*.

The Canadian government's postwar policy towards Japanese Canadians was premised on the dispersal of the population, in order to ward off any organization into groups, and to prevent the rebuilding of the Japanese–Canadian community as it had been on the west coast before the war. The result was a completely scattered community, not only geographically but psychologically. The consequent rupture between the generations was inevitable, and communication from one region to the other had ceased. If any consensus existed during the redress movement, it was limited to the concerns of the Issei. They were the victims who had borne the full force of the blows, and who wanted to get things over with the government, by any means possible.

It was the Sansei who took the lead in the National Association of Japanese Canadians, the centre of redress activity. Not only was this young generation superior in its energy; it was a generation steeped in the techniques of participation in the political process. They were confident of being able to move politicians and public opinion, and to press their demands on the government. They were able to proceed to Ottawa, and fearlessly engage in lobbying activity. Unfortunately, they may have been unable to fulfil their original purposes because of a lack of funds. However, perhaps the most important point, their skill in using the mass media was a considerable factor. Their psychological ability came naturally from having been born and raised completely within the systems of this country.

Redress was a movement which the Issei could not participate in, even if they had wanted to. That was extremely distressing to me, as an observer. The Issei had experience in forming organizations. In prewar Japanese–Canadian society, many groups were established in many localities, and a number of people distinguished themselves by their leadership. Since they had the common destiny of fighting the racial prejudices of the surrounding society, they were no doubt forced to group together for the sake of self-protection. They conducted vigorous activities, such as fund-raising, exclusively within the community, and it seems their goals were always reached. If their struggles were not directed towards the society outside, it was because their first priority was to protect themselves.

By the time the redress movement had begun, the position and the role of the Issei had vanished. Although they said it was best to leave everything to the Sansei, some were certainly dissatisfied that their opinions were not being heeded. Their pride would not let them be manipulated into behaving just as the Sansei wanted them to. That is why the old people remained so astonishingly calm when news came that the negotiations with the government had borne fruit, that a settlement had been reached, and the demands had been largely met.

There was none of the excitement of a lengthy campaign finally coming to a resolution. A few days after the announcement, I met with a group which had gathered in a Toronto park to play their habitual game of croquet. Completely absorbed in the match, they showed no excitement in the resolution of the redress problem. On questioning them, I got the reply, "If they're going to offer it, may as well take it," as if they were speaking of a third person. Even when they received their cheques for $21,000, their facial expressions did not change. Their grandchildren found it difficult to interpret their reaction.

Even if the money came in unexpectedly, they had no way of spending it. They were not hard up for money these days, and they expressed such opinions as: "We've been compensated by the government for years—I've been living on a pension for a long time"; "It's a waste of government expense," no doubt because this was not money they had won by levelling demands at anyone, and so they felt no gratification or deep emotion on receiving their cheques.

It was their grandchildren who understood the significance of victory in the redress movement, and who rejoiced for them. Redress was a purely Canadian, domestic question, which arose from the issue of civil rights for Japanese Canadians; its roots lay in the hateful notion of racism. The significance of the movement was to clarify the situation to Canadians in general, and to win their support.

At any rate, one movement came to an end, and eight years have already passed since "the year for commemoration above all others in Japanese–Canadian history" saw the settlement of the redress question. This year of commemoration was also the year of a clearly marked change of generations. The precursors from Japan who had first settled in this northern land more than 100 ago, the new generation who followed them, and then the Nisei, have already withdrawn from the front lines. A new community made up exclusively of the postwar "complete Canadians" is making its appearance.

The committee set up to determine how the $12,000,000 community fund is to be distributed and used, the Japanese–Canadian Redress Foundation, is composed of representatives from all over the country. But not one Issei was named to it. Evidently, no consulting role was considered for them during the rebuilding of the community. It probably did not occur to the young people. Can the vitality of the past ever return to a community which is to be rebuilt with the aid of $12,000,000? Is there a reason for the community to exist in the first place? If we try to define the group called Japanese Canadians, there is no unique culture left, no value system to differentiate it from other groups. We are living in a time when even the colour of one's skin has waned in importance as a factor distinguishing group from group.

Among the five Issei women appearing in this volume, Mrs Maki Fukushima was the only one to witness redress, and just barely at that. According to her daughter, who went every day to care for her in a special nursing home in Toronto, she was in a state of "waiting to be taken to Paradise any day now." In August 1992 she would have been 100 years old. Thus, redress had no substantial meaning for her.

I imagine that even if these five women had received the substantial amount of $21,000 compensation, they would have had no way to use it.

It was like going off to climb a golden mountain. You'd get money, then you'd just wait to go back to Japan.
                                        Mrs Maki Fukushima

2 Mrs Maki Fukushima

Mrs Maki Fukushima, born in August 1892, turned 90 this past summer. In August 1982, a special celebration was held for her; it was the customary big event for an 88th birthday. The decorations in her room included a message of congratulations from Prime Minister Trudeau which was placed beside a photograph of her late husband.

Mrs Fukushima says that her grandchildren, whom she met at the festivities after a long time, have grown up, to the point of being unrecognizable, and that they all came with their own children. On seeing them, she reflected that she had lived a very long life. She has raised five grandchildren with great care. All of them are married and have their own families. The great-grandchildren are getting so big that she cannot recognize them.

As a sign of age, her eyesight has gradually weakened, so that she needs a magnifying class to see details. Writing has become such a problem that she can barely sign her name. Even so, other than her failing eyesight, she has no physical problems. She attributes her good health to the exercises she has devised for herself, that she does every morning. On fine days, she enjoys going into the garden, where she moves about as she likes, watering and weeding the plants.

Mrs Fukushima lives in an old-age home for Japanese Canadians called the Nipponia Home, in a small town about 90 miles from Toronto. She has been a resident for approximately 20 years. Almost everybody else who entered the home when she did has died, and so she is now one of the few senior members. When she decided to come 20 years ago, it seems she was in the pink of health, so vigorous that it was hard to call her old, and everyone around her was amazed. Mrs Fukushima made the decision herself. Since she was nearing 70 and her task of bringing up her grandchildren was over, she thought it best to retire to the country. Brushing aside the strong objections of her family, she left her son's house in Toronto, where she had been living.

Entering a home at this stage, by her own choice, proved an extremely good decision for Mrs Fukushima. She thinks that above all else, she did well to free herself psychologically from her family. Her monthly widow's pension and the old-age pension cover the charges of the home, and leave even a small sum for pocket money. Thinking that she would like to help out with chores in the home, to be of service in some way, she has willingly taken on such jobs as caring for sick people. The home also has a large vegetable garden, and since Mrs Fukushima has grown vegetables for a long time, she continues to do it, even now.

Every morning, Mrs Fukushima invariably goes to check on those of her neighbours who have become weaker than she is. She helps those who are losing their mental or physical faculties by changing their clothes and taking them to the washroom. At this home, the custom is for everybody to assemble in the dining hall to say good morning. Mrs Fukushima says that until she becomes unable to leave her bed, she wants to encourage her fellow residents and take them to the dining hall. Not that anyone has ever asked her for help, but she believes this to be a daily task left for her, and she is carrying it out faithfully. At five am she is out of bed, takes time to do her exercises, and after seeing to her neighbours, she eats breakfast. Such is her daily schedule, and evidently it is one cause of her good health and longevity.

Her three children, who are all equally considerate of her, live in Toronto, and visit about once a month. This is gratifying in itself, but life in the country is "like living in Heaven," and she is deeply contented. It has been 40 years since her husband died, but Mrs Fukushima can say sincerely that she has become accustomed to solitude, and that she suffers not at all from being alone. She is spending her last years in peace, "grateful for whatever happens."

A reticent woman, Mrs Fukushima speaks frankly, though without exaggeration, and integrity underlies her every word. Her memory is amazingly accurate, and she relates many details. I find it pleasant to listen to her speaking in the accents of her native district, the Chugoku area, but she seemed to be trying to speak to me in her "Sunday best," or standard Japanese.

Mrs Maki Fukushima comes from Shitada, Towa-cho, Oshima-gun, in Yamaguchi Prefecture. Oshima is also known as Yashiro-jima, and as its name "big island" implies, it is quite sizable. It is the third largest island of the Inland Sea, after Awajishima and Shodojima. From Obatake Station on the Sanyo Line, the Oshima Bridge joining the island to the Honshu mainland can be seen. Today, this bridge permits easy access to the island by car. Under the bridge runs the current called the Oshima Seto, rapids which until very recent times were considered so dangerous that no bridge could be built over them. In 1976 the kilometre-long bridge was completed, and it is now very convenient to live on the island.

A bus ride from Obatake Station, around the coast of the island, takes half a day. Low mountain ranges run over the whole island; the mountaintops afford a splendid view of the islands of the Inland Sea, the mountains of Shikoku, and the city of Matsuyama. I remembered Mrs Fukushima's words: "In Towa-cho, where I was born, there's a mountain called Shirakisan, and for a child, there was nothing in the world like the view from the top of that mountain." She added that "it was such a poor island that the only thing you could brag about was the scenery," but now, Oshima is making efforts to turn that scenery to profit through the tourist industry. The islanders are engaged mainly in tourism or growing mandarin oranges, and there is also the old tradition of going away to do migrant work.

Thanks to the bridge, it has become possible to live on the island and commute to work on the mainland. That is why young people, who had gone to work in Hiroshima or Osaka, have recently returned to Oshima. Morning and night, the many twisting roads of the island are filled with the cars of commuters. Since their native island is so calm and beautiful, many of them want to come back, as long as it is possible to make an ordinary living. Perhaps Mrs Fukushima, too, has such thoughts occasionally.

Oshima, although a scenically beautiful island, is, historically, a place that people have had to leave to find migrant work in order to survive. Yataro Doi, the author of *A History of Emigration to Hawaii from Oshima-gun, Yamaguchi Prefecture*[1], explains that emigration to Hawaii from the island began as an extension of the custom of migrant work which had been carried on for a very long time. Basically, Oshima consists of mountains and hills, with little arable land. With the coming of modern times, the population grew to the point that not enough food could be produced

---

[1] Yataro Doi, *A History of Emigration to Hawaii from Oshima-gun, Yamaguchi Prefecture*, Tokuyama-shi, Yamaguchi-ken, Matsuno Shoten, 1980.

locally to support it. The men left to engage in migrant work as carpenters, stonemasons, or sailors, and the women stayed at home, barely surviving by weaving cotton fabrics.

From 1877 to 1887, Oshima was caught in the pinch of hard times, and many of the men, laid off from their migrant jobs, came home. On top of that, the island was struck by the natural calamities of storm and flood, and for a time it appeared to be threatened with near-starvation.

Thus in 1884, when the first announcement of applications for passage to Hawaii came out, candidates from Oshima rushed to fill them out. This was the first time there were government-sponsored contracts for emigration. The Japanese government formulated a policy of calling for applications from areas with high-density populations where making a living was the difficult. In Yamaguchi Prefecture, for better or worse, Oshima-gun was singled out as one of these areas: an indication of how destitute Oshima was known to be at that time. The subprefectural and village administrations encouraged emigration, making great efforts to get applicants.

Local histories record that the entire island came to grips with the issue of emigration. When the first shipload of migrant workers set out for Hawaii, 30 per cent of the 944 men were from Oshima-gun. Obviously the method of dealing with emigration was not uniform throughout all the regions. Among the islanders, appealing stories about migration spread by word of mouth, and it came about that emigrants left each year from every part of the island. Thus Oshima-gun became a precursor for regions sending emigrants to Hawaii and North America. Until 1894, when the system of government-contract emigration was abolished, Yamaguchi Prefecture ranked with Hiroshima Prefecture as the source of the greatest number of emigrants. Detailed statistics in Doi's work make it clear that the largest percentage of emigrants came from the three eastern subprefectures of Oshima, Kuga and Kumage.

As the years passed, the way emigrants departed changed: first they went by government contract; later they had individual contracts, no contracts, or relatives would send for them. Whatever the form, for about 40 years, until emigration to North America almost dried up in the late 1920s, a steady stream of emigrants left Oshima-gun.

There must have been a considerable number of people who crossed and recrossed the Pacific Ocean, and they most probably brought back considerable amounts of money to the island. Looking at the Oshima of today, there is no telling how greatly the toil and suffering of the emigrants affected the lives of the people of the island. Emigration, in the form of temporary labour, has become a far-off memory even for the old people, who muse "now that I think of it, that's what happened in the old days." It has left no traces, no matter where one looks on the island, and no matter with whom one speaks. This absence is extremely curious.

I wish I was better at talking.

Oshima-gun in Yamaguchi Prefecture used to be called Yashirojima, and it's a big island. The place I come from is called "Towa-cho" now, but it used to be "Towa-son"; it's like all the other villages that got renamed, from "son" to "cho." There were fishermen, too, but it was really a farm village. People grew things like rice and sweet potatoes, and it was just a little village, so they weren't sent out to be sold, and we hardly managed to get enough to eat. In those days everybody ate a vegetable diet, but on the island they used to catch some good sardines. Anyway, we ate things like that too, so nobody was really dirt poor. In farm families, even if there was enough rice for meals, they'd be mixed in barley, to make half rice and half barley, and then there were sweet potatoes. Some people left to work in other parts of Japan, but from my village, not many went overseas. I think that was because we could get along without going abroad.

My people were farmers until my father's generation; he quit farming and went into business. In the old days, there used to be little wooden boats going between the island and the mainland, but around the time I was born, they'd use steamboats. And my father was a shipping agent. Basically, he was in transport, but between times he used to sell things retail, like fertilizer or cigarettes. He'd sold all his land and put the money into the business, but by the time I was growing up, the business was starting to go downhill.

There was a primary school in our village, but Komatsu-cho, another village on the island, it was the biggest one, had a merchant marine school. It was well-known even in other parts of Japan. To go to middle school or a girls' school, you had to leave the island and go to Yamaguchi. I went to the primary school in the village until the sixth grade, then I went to night school. My father wanted to give his children an education, but the family was starting to go bankrupt, and as the head of the household he had to consider the neighbourhood and the relatives, so he couldn't send us to school. Then, he talked to a schoolteacher, who organized a night school for us. Four or five of us got lessons in abacus, reading, writing, and ethics, by the light of a coal lamp. Personally, it didn't amount to much at all, and that's why I'm uneducated. How couldn't I be?

I'm sure that when I was born, in 1892, there was compulsory education. But the people in the village never used writing, so they thought they didn't need an education. Around then, a lot of the women hadn't ever gone to school. When I was seven, and started school, there were children three or four years older who started coming to school too, thinking they would like to learn how to write a letter at least, even in the simplest words. And some girls came to school carrying small children, their younger siblings, on their backs.

In those days, people thought fourth grade was enough schooling. Then, if it was boys, they'd go and learn a trade like carpentry, or they'd go into the army. My older brother went through the higher grades, and boarded in the village doctor's house while he went to night school. He was healthy then, but when he was 25, in Osaka, he got sick from beriberi, and when it went to his chest, he died.

A girl might work as farmhouse help, or as a weaver. There was a weaver's shop and they gave us work there, and you would weave things to sell, and your own clothes. As for sewing, you went to a sewing teacher. I was the oldest of five girls, and with my brother, the one that died, there were six of us. My sisters are 70, 80 now, and all living. We're all long-lived in our family.

When I was growing up, there was just a steamboat to the island, and I'd never seen a train. It was really a pretty island. Until I went overseas, I'd never been away from the island. That was when I had my first train ride, too. The only places I knew were the village where I was born, and the one my husband came from, and I'd never gone to the tip of the island. If people were going off the island, they only went about as far as the Kompira

Shrine in Shikoku to pay their respects, or the Miyajima Shrine in Hiroshima Prefecture.

When women left the island to work, they went as maids, and a lot of them did that when they were around my age. My family was in business, so I wasn't allowed to go. That shows you how much everybody wanted to leave. Girls of 17 or 18 from other villages would leave home, and get onto the steamboats my family ran. They'd come at night, in groups of three or so, and leave on the morning boat. I often heard my father telling them: "Some girls get fooled by employment agencies, and then they're sold to brothels, so don't let that happen to you." It did happen that girls got fooled, and sold. You heard stories like parents going to look for a girl, when she'd already been taken to a brothel. About all the work you could find if you left the island was domestic service, or you could go to a silk mill.

From our village, two of us came to Canada. Besides me, there was Mrs Nakamura; she was three years older. She's healthy even now. In some parts of Oshima-gun, a lot of people emigrated to Hawaii or Canada, depending on the village. I'd heard tell of people from my village who'd gone to Hawaii. My cousin had gone, too. But if you looked at the whole village, there weren't many emigrants. When I look back on it, we could get along without going overseas, so it must have been a better-off village than others.

I wanted like anything to go to America, even though I couldn't have known a thing about the country. My cousin was in Seattle, and he was running a big business with his wife. We wrote to each other, and it seemed America was such a good place to live that I started wanting to go. In school I didn't learn much, and that meant geography too, so I thought America and England and places like that were all near each other, and Canada was in America, like Seattle. When I got married and came, I found Canada wasn't America. I was told to look at my passport, and it said Canada was a British territory. That was when I found out; it was a big shock.

My cousin had gone from Hawaii to the U.S. and was working in tailoring and sundries, and in his photos, he looked as if he was really living in style. He talked big, like saying he saved ten dollars a day, and that's why I started wanting to go. He left the village at a very early time. I was just a child: I guess it was around 1897 when he left.

My husband's village was about three miles from mine, and people there heard that I wanted to go to America. My husband's parents came around, saying that it was just about time for their son to get married, so our parents decided on it. I was still only 18 years old. I didn't know what kind of man he was, but I was happy as long as I could get to America. It was easy to make money in America. My family was poor, and it was going bankrupt, and anybody could see my parents were just making do with what they had. I started feeling they were in a bad way, and wanted go somewhere to make money and help them out, and not bother to get married. I had so many younger sisters, you see. I was just an innocent girl, not even 19 years old, and thought I'd like to make money. I'd work very hard and save lots of money.

My parents didn't try to stop me from going, in fact, they told me to go and do my very best, and then come back. My father was on the progressive side, so he didn't object. My grandmother didn't, either. She even said: "Going to America is like going to climb a golden mountain. So I'll wait for you to come back with money." She died when she was 84. My husband's grandmother said: "You're coming back soon, so don't be sad; just go. And you're not to cry when you leave." So everybody sent me off, encouraging me.

I got married without meeting my husband once. I didn't have any idea what kind of man he was, or what kind of work he was doing in Canada, or how he lived. I was nearly 19 and he was 30, so there was an 11-year difference. He'd come to Canada in 1899 at the age of 17. When we got married, he was still waiting to hear about his application for a temporary draft exemption. There was a man in Victoria, an uncle, and through him, four brothers in the family had come to Canada, one after the other. So he came at age 17, and after ten years and more, he finally got married to me. It isn't that he made money and sent for me. He did send my parents money for my travel expenses, but he may have borrowed it. That's what I think now, looking back on it after all these years.

There was a sort of wedding ceremony without the bridegroom; it was held at my husband's house, and they put my name into the Fukushima family register. Then I waited to go. After six months I got my passport and just at that time, my husband's younger brother and a friend of his both found wives, and so all three of us brides left the village together. My father took me all the way to Kobe. I was dressed Japanese-style in a *hakama*, a divided skirt. The reason for the divided skirt was, I thought that it would look very bad if I wore a kimono and the hem didn't stay down, for example when I got on the boat.

If I think of the feelings I had in those days, I wasn't hoping for anything very wonderful. All I wanted to do was to go and see America, so it wasn't anything specially emotional. I didn't even wonder what would happen if I didn't like my husband. I didn't even discuss it with my friends. I didn't have any idea that I'd like or dislike my husband. I thought it was all right because my parents approved. When you get used to people, you end up getting attached to them, and so you can put up with them. It doesn't matter if you get married just through pictures, or if you get married after meeting the man, it depends on how you act, for the marriage to become a success.

I left Japan at the end of December 1913, and New Year's Day came halfway through the trip; I got to Victoria in January of the next year. It was a 6,000-ton, Japanese merchant ship called the *Canada Maru*, and it pitched a lot because it was right in the middle of winter, but I didn't have any feeling I'd come through a terrible experience. At the time, a 20-year old girl was very naive, and even if she was suffering, she couldn't say anything about it. I was going as a bride, but I only had a little bedding and nightwear, and only a few extra clothes. My father bought me a blanket in Kobe because he thought it would get cold when the boat went through the Russian Sea. As for English, I came without knowing a word, not even "yes" or "no." I didn't study it at all beforehand.

When we landed in Victoria, I met my husband for the first time. I didn't have any particular feeling when I saw him. I wasn't excited about it, because I didn't have any idea of being married. I felt the same as if I'd been at home in Japan. He bought me an outfit of Western clothes, and we announced the marriage to the people he knew at the immigration centre, and then we went to Vancouver the next day.

At that time, my husband had a contract piling up ties in a sawmill that made them for railway lines, on a mountain called something like Tamsend or Townsend, five miles from New Westminster. It happened to be a snowy winter, and after we took the train from Vancouver to New Westminster, we walked along the train tracks. I thought the snow was awfully deep. It was all new to me, because Yamaguchi is a warm place, and it doesn't snow.

We got to the camp, and it was such a filthy place. I was told to go into the bunkhouse. When I did, I could see the sky through the cracks in the ceiling. You heated the place by putting big pieces of firewood in the stove, but that was a worry because it might cause a fire. I thought, oh what a miserable place, there's nothing like this in Oshima, so how can there be one in America? But I didn't have time to think about being surprised. There was work to do right away. The very next morning I got up at four and worked at cooking and washing. I couldn't stand it, and before ten days were up, I was saying over and over "let me go back to Japan, please, let me go back." That was impossible, and seven months after I got there, the tie loading was finished, and we left camp. By then, I'd become completely resigned.

In this camp, there were about 10 men from Oshima. My husband had come when he was young, so even though all he spoke was broken English, he could get along. He even interpreted quite a bit for his friends. So he got to be sort of a subcontractor that worked in different camps; he'd get together the men he knew, and arrange contracts.

My husband had quite a good nature. He did have a bent for playing cards and gambling, but after he married me, it was just once in a while, and as for drinking, it was just social. So there was nothing wrong with my husband, but he hadn't saved any money. Working in a camp is a terrible way to make a living. I realized I had made a big mistake when I was in Japan and thought money grew on trees in America. I didn't know anything when I came, so I was quick to change my mind, too. I thought, oh well, this is the way things are, and I didn't care any more. My husband came from a farm, so he could do anything. It seems he used to work on the railway, and fishing boats, and he would never say he couldn't do something. He worked hard and there was never a time I lacked for spending money.

Once tie-stacking was over in July we went to Steveston. My husband had been asked to go by his salmon-fishing partner, and they went out fishing. It was a year when the sockeye catch was very good, and I was a day worker at the cannery. It was salmon canning. What you did was take the bones out beside the machines, and you flattened out the pieces of salmon to put them in the cans. If it was piecework, at two dozen cans per box, you could pack 150 boxes a day, and for 150 boxes you got ten dollars, I think. If you worked by the hour, they gave you 35 cents. I remember it was the first work where I made money, since coming from Japan. We stayed in a boarding house that was run by people from Hiroshima Prefecture, and sometimes, when there was more fish than usual being caught, I'd go to the cannery at seven in the morning, and work till eleven at night.

In October the fishing ended and we went back to Vancouver. At that time, I was pregnant. Our oldest son was born the next year, and three years later, our second son. In that time we were doing different things, like working in plants where they smoked and salted herring, or going into the mountains, or fishing, and we went on for seven years like that. Japanese didn't have fixed work then, and they'd keep changing jobs. I didn't speak English, so all I did was follow my husband. As I went along, I was in charge of the cooking and laundry. Whenever we moved, we'd take a lot of baggage with us, like cooking gear: a big pot to boil rice in for the people that worked for us. Wherever we went, I'd work alongside of my husband, looking after the children.

When one job was finished, my husband would go to the mountains and look for another. He got helped out by eight, ten people from our part of Japan, and he'd do contract work in lumbering, mostly. The year after I came, we went to Vancouver Island, and worked in a herring plant. We'd skin the herrings and smoke them, then take off the heads and tails, and pack them in boxes to send to England or Europe. This was another contract job my husband got; the wages came to 50 cents an hour. After the herring plant, we went to a place called Port Alberni, and worked at salting herring. This went on for another year or two.

Around the time when our oldest son was starting to walk, we went into wild mountain country where nobody had ever been before. That was a time when we really suffered. We were in a place, an island chain called something like Tobins or Toba; even now I don't know where it is. You took a ferry from Vancouver to a place near the island, and a boat from there. The work was to cut down all the trees on a mountain. The manager took about 40 of us to the mountains. My brother-in-law and his wife were in the crew, and she was going as a cook, like me. We'd been influenced to go by my brother-in-law, and my husband had turned down another job for this one. We spent all the money we'd earned from the herring work and laid in some food.

We were in the advance work crew, and got off the boat onto the beach, and lived in tents. We went up a mile and pitched tents again, then two miles on, we slept in a tent-house. The kitchen was in the tent-house. At the fourth stage, we slept in a log house. After one more mile, we built the houses we were going to stay in. So it was the fifth stage up from the beach, half-way up the mountain, that we settled in. I think it was October. At night the wolves howled; they were called coyotes. It was a lonely place, and when it snowed, it came down thick and fast. There were mountains all around, and no wind. Most of the people in the crew were from Oshima, with a few from other prefectures. In one row there was a young wife who'd just come from Japan, and it was her first time in a place like this, so I felt sorry for her. But she was well-behaved, and didn't mope.

There were really some beautiful trees on the mountain. The manager made the contracts, and his plan was that in spring the lumber already cut down would be taken into the valley and the thawing snow would float it out to sea naturally. This man was our friend too. If he'd succeeded it would have been a fine piece of work. But the plan failed badly, because the melting snow didn't flow down into the valley—that was the lay of the land. Nobody had ever come to this mountain before. Anybody that did come would have given up soon and gone home.

It was October when we went to the mountain, and winter came soon. As we were in a tent house, there was no cooking space, so I'd get up early in the morning and follow my sister-in-law outside, and we'd cook meals in the rain and snow for dozens of people. The men built everything in a hurry, what 40 or 50 people needed for sleeping space, toilets, bath and kitchen. There weren't even proper boards; they cut shingles from around there, using hatchets, to build the houses. They'd level cliffs and pave trails and make toilets here and there. As for the bathhouse, you had to go three blocks uphill. And when you got out of the bath, the towel would go stiff from the cold. That's how cold it was. The men had some really dangerous experiences. That was something that went with working in the mountains in those days. It was lucky if nobody got hurt, or sick. Everyone in our crew did their best and we were lucky that nobody even caught a cold.

As for the food, all we had was what we brought, and what we ordered in once in a while, so there was nothing fresh, like vegetables. At New Year's we thought we'd have a treat and ordered in some materials to make sushi with, but the horse slipped on the way, and fell into the valley, so the load was ruined. I had ordered a present for my older son too, a big can full of some rice-crackers, but that fell into the valley too, and the can got squashed flat. And other Japanese food that was hard to get, like dried gourd and laver, everything got ruined. I was so sorry.

Then in springtime, when the thaw came, we found out that the water wouldn't flow down into the valley, so the whole thing went bust and we had to go home, but I was really glad. We'd spent over half a year on that big job and sunk all our money into it, and when we went down the mountain we didn't have a penny. Everybody went bust.

At the time, my parents were worried and they kept writing me. They wrote because they wondered how we were doing in a strange place nobody had ever heard of. Every time I read those letters I cried. It made me nostalgic, and I was so happy to get the letters, even though I could hardly read my father's handwriting; it was the old-fashioned "temple-school" style.

When I wrote a letter telling them that I got up every morning at four o'clock and cooked for dozens of people, my husband said I mustn't write anything like that. He said that he wouldn't look good if my parents thought we couldn't manage unless I did anything like that, so he didn't let me write. As for saving up enough money to help my parents out, that was completely out of the question. Then my parents sent word that it would be a bother if people started to say their daughter who'd gone to America was sending them lots of money, so they wouldn't let me send any. My mother-in-law was living alone, though, so we were mailing her some spending money, maybe $10, $15 at a time.

In 1920, after we'd been married seven years, I went back to Japan with my husband and the two boys, and I was pregnant with my third child. My husband hadn't been back in 20 years.

He went back to Canada a few months later, but I had the baby in Japan and was still nursing it, so I stayed on for about a year and a half, then I left the three children with my mother and went back to Canada.

By getting the children looked after, we'd both be free to work, we thought, and we really would save up some money this time. We were a couple the same as before, going out to work on the fishing grounds or in the mountains. Soon after we got back, I went to Hammond alone to work at strawberry picking. I wasn't willing, but I worked about ten hours a day, for 50 days. The same as before, we went from place to place to find work.

I didn't have the children around now, so while we were in Vancouver, I went to night school and began to study English for the first time in my life. I was taken there by a friend. I finished Book One, and got to be able to read some street names.

Before three years had gone by, my mother who was looking after the children got sick, and my husband and I hurried back to Oshima. The children had become used to Japan, and said they didn't want to go to America. So I had a house built in my home town, and lived there with the three children. My husband had gone back alone and sent money for our living expenses every time he saved something. This went on for two or three years. The house he had built for me is still standing. Later, during the war, when my husband had died, it occurred to me that I might like to go back to Japan, and that was because of the house.

We had come to Canada meaning to do temporary work and go back after three or five years, and we did all kinds of work, thinking to save money. We went back and forth, to and from Japan, and didn't settle down here until I came back with the children in 1927. We were concentrating on going back to Japan, so the money we worked for was spent on travel, and for the passage alone, the cheapest you could get was $55, and the average was about $65. Once I took the special rate "deluxe third class," and that cost $135. My husband really worked, too. He had enough money to build that house in Japan, so he certainly made a bit. But I'm sorry to say that the migrant worker spirit really wasn't good.

When I came back with the children, we settled in Vancouver. My husband was working for himself as a gardener then. Our oldest son had gone through Grade Six in Japan, the second through Grade 3, and the smallest, Grade 1. They didn't speak English at all, so the oldest had to go to Grade 1 English. He had a hard time getting used to Canada, and he felt bad. I felt sorry for him, too. He said that he didn't want to go to school with little kids, and that he hated school. After the year at public school, he wouldn't go on to the upper grade, no matter how much I begged him to. As he didn't mind going to an auto mechanics' school, I encouraged him to do that, even though there weren't many cars around at the time.

About then the Depression hit, and those were really bad times. My husband had settled on gardening, and there was always some kind of work, so we never wanted for food, but the children had been brought back with no clothes to speak of, and they had to be dressed from head to toe, and they had to go to school. So I took somebody's advice and went to work as a housekeeper. We talked about it the night I came back from Japan, and the next day, even without knowing English, I left my own house and went to work. My friend took me along: I learned what to do, and I kept doing housework in Vancouver right up to the war.

We were living in the Fairview district of Vancouver. There was a sawmill, so lots of Japanese lived in the area. If you worked as a couple, you could get along even during the worst of the Depression. You could eat and pay for things in stores without going into debt. We weren't badly off in Vancouver.

A lot of our friends had trouble. One had five or six children, and her husband was a carpenter, but the jobs ran out completely. These people were really Japanese, and said they wouldn't go on relief, even if it meant going into debt. A debt, that was something you could pay off some day, but if you accepted relief, then you would shame even your children. So their rent piled up for two or three years, and they bought all their food on credit. The store owners didn't even frown; they gave credit for a year or two. On the other hand, these people were very honest and loyal, so even if there were sales at other stores, they wouldn't shop in them.

I started out doing day work. I'd spend the whole day cleaning, washing and ironing. I went around to a different house every day. At the places where we worked, a gardener got 45 cents an hour, and the men that worked for my husband got 37 to 40 cents; those were the going rates. When he was busy, he hired two or three helpers. My housework lasted from nine to four, and I got $2.50 a day plus two streetcar tickets. If you lived in, you got $30 to $40 a month. At the time, 100 pounds of rice cost $4.50 or $5.00, and that was good rice from Japan.

After a while, we went to work as a couple in the house of some white people where my husband had been the gardener. I worked there till we left Vancouver when the war began, it was maybe 12 or 13 years in all. They were very nice to us. To make up for not knowing English, I worked hard, so they took good care of me. To please them, I was willing to work, and even when it was time to stop, I kept at the job till it was done. They would have confirmed that. When the Mrs wasn't feeling well and her shoulders were stiff, I'd give her a massage, then she'd get well again. She'd tell her friends and everybody about it.

When the war came and we had to move, we stopped working. They were really sorry and both of them said we didn't have to leave. The husband was even a member of the legislature, and as an individual, he was a very fine person. If you go out to work as a gardener or housekeeper, and you get to know the inside of a house, and know the people well, then they start doing things for you. Though when it comes to associating with whites, people like us could only meet them through work.

Once there was an election, and our boss was a candidate. Then, he asked my husband to stop gardening for him, just during the campaign. He must have thought it was a handicap if people saw that he had a Japanese working for him. My husband got very angry. He said if he was going to be discriminated against like that, he'd never go and work there again, no matter how much he was begged to. After the election, the Mrs asked me if I would get my husband to come back. In the end, he didn't, but it's sure there was discrimination everywhere.

The Japanese probably got excluded because they worked too hard. That was the trouble. They got in the way of the whites. If it was fishing, the Japanese would be at it all the time. That's why they caught more than enough fish. No wonder they got in the way of white people. We liked working more than money. Since we didn't understand the language, we worked as hard as we could. The bosses were pleased with that. And then we got into competition with the whites. The Japanese all worked hard, so hard that they almost begrudged the time it took to smoke a cigarette. Even so, they didn't ask for more wages than they were getting. Me, I used to work past five o'clock even when I didn't have to. If the work wasn't finished then, I didn't go home until it was done. But for all that, I didn't get overtime.

When I worked as a housekeeper, that's when I got closest to English, but when you just clean the house and do the washing, you don't need words. You get there and say "Good morning" and when you leave "Goodbye", and for the rest, you can get along without saying anything. If you're smart, you learn conversation. But we didn't want to say the words wrong, and it's not in my nature to push. Even if I say things the way they're written down, the other person doesn't understand. I can guess what the other person is saying more or less, but I don't understand exactly.

The children were brought up in Japan, so they have no trouble with Japanese. What they do have trouble with is English. When I look back on it now, it was a very bad idea to take them to Japan. I think it was a foolish thing to do. We couldn't think of anything but going back to Japan. We certainly didn't think there would be a war, and there was no way we thought we would ever move east. We didn't see into the future.

After coming back from Japan in 1927, I settled down, and never thought of going back again. The year after I got back, all of us were baptized as Christians. The children had started Sunday School, and they were saying they wanted to be baptized. As I didn't know anything about Christ, I said no, but the Sunday School teacher and some believers talked me into it. I went along with them and got baptized without understanding anything. The children believed in Christianity, but we didn't have any religion to speak of, so I decided to follow the children. I thought that as long as we were in this country, its religion would be good.

So I went along with the children, with no deep thought. I urged my husband to get baptized, but he wouldn't. So just the four of us were baptized, but it happened that through somebody else persuading him, my husband got baptized too, in the same year. So the whole family became Christians. There was a Japanese church in Fairview, and that's where we went. We were under a Japanese pastor. Going to church on Sunday was a real treat, because we didn't have any amusements. My social life was just with Japanese, and among them, people from the same prefecture, then among those, people from the same subprefecture, Oshima.

My husband died about a month after the war began. It began on December 7, 1941, and at the time he wasn't naturalized, so he was classified as an enemy alien. Then he got sick right away. He'd been a healthy person, and was never sick, but he caught a slight cold, his heart got worse, and he suffered because of asthma, and so I put him in hospital. There weren't many nurses because of the war, so after I finished my housekeeping job, I went to the hospital around five o'clock to look after him. As I walked along the street, I kept getting called awful names, "Jap, Jap." I was terribly scared of getting on the streetcar, and I went back and forth thinking how much I hated it.

My husband kept insisting he wanted to go home, but in three weeks he died. It was the 26th of January 1942. I certainly wasn't glad that he died, but I did manage to give him a proper funeral right at the beginning of the war. If it had turned out that we had to go away leaving him behind, sick, and if he were going to die anyway, it was better for him to die then. He was 61 years old. His 60th birthday, we held it inside the family, but the children said it wasn't a good idea, and that's why they didn't have a celebration for my 60th.

Soon we had our move from Vancouver hanging over us, and so I wasn't sad or lonely because my husband had died. All I could think of was where to go after this, so there was no time to think about him.

In wartime, all kinds of rumours were circulating. Some people said that if young people were sent to the camps out east, they might have to go to war. At the time, my oldest son had a wife and a baby. I thought it would be too sad if they were separated, and we thought of a place where we could all go together. We didn't have the money to move where we wanted. So we applied for sugar beet growing in Alberta, where we could go as a family.

The people around me didn't have anything good to say about our going to the sugar beet fields. My husband's best friend said "You shouldn't go to work on beets. It's like being a traitor." Making sugar out of beets meant cooperating with the Canadian government that had a policy to produce more sugar. It would be like making bullets for rifles or a sign of loyalty to this country.

I said "We're going to the sugar beet fields, because we decided that's how we can go as a family. The last thing we'd do is aim a rifle at Japan. I've got a Rising Sun flag in my heart," and off we went. We'd never farmed, so that was a worry, but we went because we'd be together. The Japanese all had different ways of thinking, and coping with things, but we were about the only family that went from Fairview to Alberta; I didn't know what else to do.

My husband had died in January and we left Vancouver in May. My second son was working as a book-keeper in the Fraser

Valley Farmers' Association. He sacrificed himself and took everybody along with him to Alberta. He was 22 or 23. At the time I wasn't naturalized, so I was an "Enemy Alien." In the late 1920s, the thinking generally was that there shouldn't be any extra Japanese around, and after it looked like a war was coming, it wasn't easy to get naturalized.

We were in Alberta four years, all during the war, and had a terrible time. When we were on the train leaving New Westminster, a telegram came. It said they didn't need any more Japanese. We'd cleared out our house, so even if we were told to go home, there wasn't any home to go to. So we went off just as we were. We got to Lethbridge in Alberta, after two whole days in the train. Nobody came to meet us, no bosses. They didn't want any Japanese coming. Then it got to be like being sold as slaves. We got taken all across Alberta from west to east, stopping at every station, and family after family got sold off.

We were just five adults and a baby, but we weren't farmers so it was very hard to find a buyer. We were leftover goods, and got sold at the very end. Nowadays, there's oil in Alberta, but then, it was nothing but poor farming villages. The one we went to, I forget its name, but it was a small, poor village. It was a cold place, not good for beets. Right away, we planted seeds, but they didn't grow well. July came, but now it was too hot and the beets grew and grew, it was earth that you couldn't grow daikon radish in, but it was good for leaves. We broke our backs working, but we failed.

The first year we got treated like enemies, and the people hated us. But after that year, they realized that Japanese were hard workers, and honest too, so they took a liking to us, and when you said, "All right, we're leaving the fields," now they wouldn't let us. The bosses just wouldn't sign the papers. Their beet-field labour would dry up, so they wouldn't let us leave the province. There was a sugar shortage in wartime, so they had to get beets grown. There was no work at all besides beet growing, and the young people started wanting to go east. My second son applied to the B. C. Security Commission, and at last he got permission to leave.

We failed the first year, and got money from the Commission for what we'd worked for, but the little money we had on hand, we spent. In the second year we went to the Raymond area, and grew beets on about 20 acres. You were paid 33 dollars per acre for weeding, thinning, fertilizing, and harvesting. It was terribly hard labour, and they say eight acres was all an experienced man could handle. Everybody came to help and somehow we got the harvest out, but our income was very low. Besides that, we could go to the town for day work, and my oldest son worked in a garage to earn some extra money and with some help from the Commission, somehow we had enough to eat and that's how we survived.

In the Raymond area, there were quite a few Japanese living there from before the war, but they said that during the Depression, they suffered too. Even if they wanted to feed their children rice, they had trouble finding the money to buy it. But now, the leftover wheat went out for the war effort, so money came in. Some people said "We're sorry for you, but we're all right now, thanks to the war." Here and there were people like us who had come from the West Coast, but they lived in farmhouses, and "next door" could mean one or two miles away. You trudged over to visit, and spent the night.

After the war, Alberta became a really good place to live. My sons' friends all grew up and made successes of themselves. People tried to persuade us to stay there too, but we didn't have any farm experience, so we had to come east, looking for work. A lot of the people who stayed behind had been farmers in B.C. So they're all doing really well, buying land and renting it out at the same time as they're farming. People are really strong if they have land.

We lost everything in four years. I didn't get mad. I thought it was no use. Because we were Japanese, we had to go where they said. You can't do anything else, if this isn't the country you were born in; if you're told to get out, that's what you have to do. When we left B.C., I didn't think Japan would lose the war, and I thought it would be over soon, so we left everything behind. We left the good things, that is, and only brought the junk. My feeling was to be loyal to this country. But at that time I hadn't been naturalized, so I was a citizen of an enemy country. I thought I'd go to Japan, because the children could all get along by themselves. I've got a house over there, and I didn't mind living alone.

After the war, people had all kinds of ideas about what they should do with themselves, and I had trouble deciding, too. Some people kept saying I should go to Japan, and others said: "In Japan, they've got everything ready to welcome us." But other people said: "Even if you go back to Japan, what are you going to do after the war in a small country like that?" I was at my wits' end, I didn't know where to turn, and in the end I went and signed to be repatriated. My second son was shocked at this, and came hurrying back from the east, and applied to the Mounties for a cancellation. He insisted we were in Canada, and he couldn't let his mother go back to Japan alone.

He went through all the steps to change the application, and a few months later, I got news that I could stay in Canada, so my problem was solved. But I'd thought that if I was going to be a burden to my children, it would be better to live in Japan. But it isn't good for a family to get split up, no matter what.

After the war, I went to Montreal, where my second son had moved because of his work. My daughter had got married and was bringing up a family there too. I stayed in my daughter's house for eight or nine years, looking after the grandchildren. In 1954 my oldest son sent for me, and I came to Toronto. At his house, I didn't have anything to do except cooking and cleaning, and I went from one of my children to the other. So my work after the war was looking after the grandchildren. They got close to me and even when I spoke Japanese they understood. A year after I came to Toronto, my daughter came too, with her family.

All that time, the grandchildren were getting bigger and bigger, and I thought they could do without me. In fact they would all be more relaxed, and that's why I came to this home.

The children were partly brought up in Japan, and so they're really considerate of their mother. They were in Japan for seven or eight years, and they seem to think like Japanese. The people they're connected with are nice, too. Both my daughters-in-law and my son-in-law, he's dead now, they've been very nice. Other people say mean things about their daughters-in-law, but mine are even nicer than my own children. I don't need spending money, but whenever they visit, they leave some for me. And they buy all kinds of things for me.

I don't miss Vancouver any more. At first, all I knew was Japan and Vancouver. When I went to Alberta, I kept thinking I had to go back to Vancouver. But when I came east and saw how it was here, how young people could find good jobs and get along really well, I thought it was a good thing we came out here, and now I'm so glad. I don't miss the west at all.

You could say the people in Vancouver are very low; if you belong to a different race, then they take away your jobs. In B.C. I was always sure that the Japanese were going to be discriminated against. I thought the children couldn't go far in the world. They would have to follow their father and become gardeners or run a little store, and that was maybe the highest they could go.

My husband was a gardener with no education himself, so he gave up on education, saying it was useless. That's why we just sent the children to high school, no further. We had our second son quit at high school, but he said he wanted to study some more and went to night school. The oldest said he'd rather learn a trade than go to high school, so he went to an auto repair school and has always worked as a mechanic. When we came east, I realized that education was useful, and I wish we'd sent them to school longer. If only I'd been wiser. In those days, even a lot of university graduates ended up working in sawmills, if they were Japanese, so I couldn't see any further than that.

I got naturalized after coming to Toronto. I'd come to think, oh well, I'm going to get permission to stay in this country, I can't do anything else. Nowadays, I can relax, and I get enough from the government every month, so I'm really grateful. And I've been getting a widow's pension since I was 65. That's why I came to this home. It's been 19 years, and I don't have a bit of trouble, because I have the pension, and I even get spending money.

So I've been living for a long time, speaking Japanese only, and I don't understand English at all. I used to be able to figure out the newspaper headlines once in a while, but after a time I gave up because I couldn't handle it. Because even after 70 years in Canada, I've managed to live just with Japanese. Just because I couldn't speak the language, I couldn't do what I wanted to: that's the kind of life it's been. For a whole 70 years I've been living here without being of any use. I wonder why on earth I ever came to this country.

But somehow, I've come out of it all right. I've never been so poor that I hit rock bottom, and thought "this is enough for me; this is the end," and I've had an ordinary life. Even in the Depression, my husband always had jobs, so we never had to borrow. After all, when times were good, we put a little aside, we went to Japan twice, and even built a house, small as it was.

In Vancouver we used to go around looking at houses, thinking we'd have to buy one because the children were growing up. There were houses we thought of buying. At the time if you paid $1,500, you could get a very nice one. We could have, with both of us working, if we'd saved $100 a year. We thought we could save some money just from the mutual fund association, so we joined up. So we saved a little, and when the time came that we could buy a house, the war began. Now I think it's a good thing we didn't buy one. Afterwards, it would have been taken away from us by the government.

We got married through photos, but that was an ordinary thing to do. You can't say it was good or bad. At first, I wondered why on earth I'd come to America. I was dying to go back to Japan, and I was sad. But it wasn't because my husband led a fast life or anything like that, and he never did a thing to make me unhappy. He was quite a bit older, and he protected me. We never had trouble in our marriage or the family, and I thought we could pick up some money in America, but we couldn't. The money just wasn't there for the taking, and to realize that, I came all this way to a foreign country where I worked like a dog.

Ever since I got my naturalization after the war, I've been a real Canadian, but I've left my Japanese citizenship as it is. To tell the truth, I haven't been devoted to Japan, and I'm not devoted to Canada either. Japan is the country where I was born and raised, so even in war, I couldn't turn against it. If something good happens to Japan, I'll be happy with the Japanese, and if it suffers, so will I. I can't turn my back on Japan, no matter what happens. But I've been living in Canada for 70 years, and the government is taking care of me, so I can't reject this country either. My home is here. Originally I was a Buddhist, but I became a Christian, and that's the religion of this country. The only worthwhile thing I've ever done is to work seriously, and even so, I've been living here all this time without being of any use to this country.

I came with a whole lot of other brides. My husband didn't even come to fetch me.

Mrs Hana Murata

3 Mrs Hana Murata

Mrs Hana Murata is now 87 years of age. She was born in May 1895 and is living alone on her pension. Not long after World War II and her resettlement in Toronto, she used all the savings she had painfully managed to gather together to buy the house she had dreamed of. She is still living there. She says she is unwilling to leave the place she has become used to, and that she is clinging to it.

With age, she has become unable to handle the repairs and the management of the house, and it is steadily decaying. From the outside, you can tell at a glance that an old person lives in this dilapidated building. Inside, the dust has collected here and there, and it looks as if it has not been cleaned for some years. For a long time, her friends and acquaintances have been urging her to enter an old age home. A home for Japanese seniors has been opened in Toronto, and somebody has even arranged for her to go there any time she wants to. Recently, she has had many days when things are hard to do, and she thinks it would be best to go into the home, but she cannot make the final decision.

Mrs Murata's house is in an old residential area, a little west of the centre of Toronto. Originally, the inhabitants were working-class people, but with the postwar immigration boom, the area has become a big immigrant district. Most of the residents are foreign-born, like Mrs Murata. The houses in the neighbourhood are affordable for immigrants, who after a few years of work, can purchase their first home. The houses fulfil the two conditions considered by immigrant workers; low prices and convenience to public transportation. It is unusual for someone to stay as long as 30 years, like Mrs Murata has. The residents, especially the young ones, move out when they find a second house, a little more desirable and on a bigger plot. In the 1950s most immigrants were from Italy or Eastern Europe, but now people from all countries have settled here.

In the last ten years or so, black immigrants from the West Indies have moved to the neighbourhood. It seems that the houses on either side of Mrs Murata's were suddenly bought one day by black people. The result among the Japanese community in the area was that property values had gone down, but Mrs Murata is not much concerned about it.

At any rate, she is trying to do her best and put off entering the old age home, if by only one day. The thought keeps her spirits up.

Once immigrants have acquired their own house, they almost invariably think of renting out their rooms. There are one or two renters in all these houses, and Mrs Murata is no exception. Except for her own room and the kitchen, she has rented out the rest of the house to two families. Therefore, although she may be the owner, in reality it is in name only, because she has no dining room or even a bedroom to call her own. Since meals are taken in the kitchen, she cannot have guests. She has lived alone for decades, putting up with this small space. She lives modestly, paying expenses like taxes and heating from the rental income, and for the rest, she depends on her pension.

Until a year or so ago, she went religiously twice a week to the neighbourhood English classes, the kind supported by the government to teach English conversation to immigrant women. But recently she finds it more and more taxing, and now she tends to skip classes. For the first time in her life she is "completely at loose ends, just fiddling around" and she can hardly bear this sense of being idle. Since she wanted to keep some order in her daily life, she had decided to force herself to go to English classes. The Japanese United Church is quite close by, so she still goes to worship every Sunday. For the present, that is probably the extent of Mrs Murata's outside activities.

Soon after coming to Canada, Mrs Murata found herself in difficult circumstances. She was then strongly influenced by a white missionary who was "really kind and saved me," and she became a Christian. Since then, she has always attended church regularly. However, since she grew up in a place with many temples, even in Shiga Prefecture which is strongly Buddhist, it seems that her feet naturally take her towards the temple, the Buddhist church in Toronto, especially on days like the anniversary of a parent's death, or at the Bon Festival. Mrs Murata does not find this at all contradictory. The two religions coexist peacefully in her mind.

At her family home in Shiga Prefecture, there is not a single person left who knows Mrs Murata, but she says she is linked to her ancestors in spirit. She believes that it is important to honour them, because she owes them her very existence. She gives offerings of money—to the Christian church she attends—on the death dates of her grandparents, parents, brother and sisters. Since one of these anniversaries comes up almost every month, she has made a chart of them and is careful not to forget them. She often complains "I've had an unhappy life because I didn't have close relations with my family." She probably feels this way because she retains a way of thinking centred on ancestor worship, a critical part of the old family system.

When she was young, both of her marriages ended unhappily, and having just turned 26, she determined to make her way alone in a foreign country. This immigrant woman, with no particular learning or education, and no resources in particular, has lived alone for 60 years. She managed to come through it, she says, because of her fighting spirit, and because of her willingness to work. She learned dressmaking as an occupation, and continued for 60 years "doing nothing but sewing."

Mrs Murata's life story, rare among the Issei, is that of a career woman. At one time, she ran a dressmaker's shop in the middle of Vancouver, with white customers only, and she worked unassisted, with all her might. Even in the case of Issei women with their own careers, contacts with white society were, as a whole, limited to the workplace. Consequently, Mrs Murata has not once gone to a place where white people gather and she has no friends who are not Japanese. She has spent her life in a corner of Japanese–Canadian society, stigmatized because of her status as a woman alone, and has worked only in order to survive. By taking Mrs Murata's life as an example, we can see how very restricted the social ascent of Issei women has been.

Mrs Hana Murata was born and raised in a place now named Ooyabu-machi in the city of Hikone, Shiga Prefecture. It was similar to Oshima in Yamaguchi Prefecture as it too was a village of emigrants. Many people came to Canada came from Shiga Prefecture, the majority of whom were from the villages formerly called Ooyabu, Hassaka, and Mitsuya-mura (now amalgamated into the city of Hikone). Therefore, emigration was concentrated in a very specific area, centring on the district of Inukami, situated on the east-central shores of Lake Biwa. Because it directly overlooks the lake, the district was called the "East Lake emigrant villages."

From Hikone Station on the Tokaido Line, it takes half an hour by bus to reach the end of the line on the lake shore. Hugging the shore are the East Lake emigrant villages. With the surge in residential building, new houses have sprung up, and the area looks like a classic suburb. No doubt it is only a matter of time before the nearby farmlands disappear, but in the old days, it was purely an agricultural district. A number of streams flow from Lake Biwa to form a river that runs through the farmland.

As I looked at the lake and the swiftly running river, I remembered hearing about the flood of 1896. Mrs Murata had told me that the great flood was the immediate reason for emigration from the villages. That year, the rainfall had been unusually heavy, and the water in the lake gradually rose. When torrents of rain fell, typhoon-like, all the rivers overflowed at the same time. The entire village zone was transformed into a lake. Now the villagers, increasingly troubled, found themselves forced to abandon their homes.

The whole east lake village belt was a flood area to begin with. This is clear from the detailed records in the local histories of floods from the Edo period[1]. Since the area was near Lake Biwa and was constantly stricken with floods, the people could not count on their rice crops and their economic life was regularly damaged. Even without the great flood, the villagers would probably have had the right frame of mind to leave their homes for another locale. Inukami-gun, alone, was a district which many people left, to work as labourers or tradespeople in the Osaka-Kobe area. Hassaka and Ooyabu were also villages where many chose overseas migration.

It is certain that the great flood of 1896 was the reason that emigration from the East Lake villages began in earnest. However, 10 years earlier in 1886, a few men from Hassaka went to Hawaii as contract labourers: the first contact the villagers had had with a foreign country. After the great flood, from 1897, emigration continued to increase, especially to Canada. Residents like Mrs Murata's father and uncle must have left right after the flood. Mrs Murata, who was born the year before, says that when she grew old enough to notice such things, it was unusual to find a family in her village without a man who had emigrated.

Those people who left in the early period had no intention of staying away permanently. They were migrant workers who left to make money at temporary jobs. But even so, they always sent for their families.

---

[1] "Studies on the East Lake Immigrant Villages," *Research Abstracts*, Faculty of Arts, Ritsumeikan University, No. 14, 1964, Ritsumeikan University, Faculty of Arts Research Center.

Customarily, a father would send for his son, and after living with him for a time, and showing him what to do, he would return to Japan. When the time came for the son to marry, he would send for a young woman, who then emigrated. Because marriage almost invariably occurred within the village community, relations between Canada and the immigrant villages never ceased. The character of an "America Village" was constituted in the East Lake area: the men went abroad for migrant work, and the women stayed in the village, looking after the family while relying on remittances from abroad. This pattern persisted until the start of World War II.

It is certain that the East Lake "America Village" profited by the money sent by its emigrants. "Though it was a remote fishing and farming village, almost all the residences had tile roofs, and it ranked at the top in the prefectural tax records up to that year, 1931; and on three occasions, it had received a certificate for full payment of national taxes." Bank savings in 1931 were reported to be more than 2,500,000 yen[2].

Mrs Murata too began sending money home immediately after she started to work, and kept up the habit after the war. Among the villagers, it was customary. There was some competition in remitting money, so that there were even people who ended up sending nearly half of their income. This may have been the habit of the "returning type of immigrant" who aims at going home in the course of time.

In a trip around the old villages of the East Lake district, I noticed the striking temple architecture, especially the tiled roofs. This region is a stronghold of Buddhism, and even when its followers went overseas, they did not forget the temples of their home towns. Every time someone sent a contribution for rebuilding a temple, or some other occasion, it meant a religious duty had been fulfilled. These fine temples may be the only surviving traces of the America Village period of the East Lake region.

Somewhere at one of these temples is the grave of Mrs Murata's ancestors. Mrs Murata, wishing to be buried with them, has prepared her own place there. She may be called the typical, returning type of immigrant, at least spiritually, and to the end.

It is winter. The village on the east shore takes the direct blasts of wind from the lake, and it falls into a cold silence. There can be no returning to the ancestral home.

---

2 Ibid., p. 166.

The place I was born is all in the city of Hikone now, but properly speaking, it was called Ooyabu in Aoyagi Village in the Inukami-gun (Subprefecture), Shiga Prefecture. You cross the bridge from Hikone, and my village is right there. It was a small place but even so there must have been 150 houses or so. A lot of people from the village have come to Canada and America. In Hassaka, the village next to ours, someone in every family had come to Canada.

My people were small farmers, and when I was a child, my father had already gone to Vancouver. The first time he went was about 100 years ago, maybe. He worked as a fisherman and sent money back to us. His brother, my uncle, had a big grocery in Vancouver, and he'd sell miso, soy sauce, and pickles that he made himself. When my uncle retired, he'd crossed the Pacific 17 times, he said. In those days everybody came for temporary work, and I remember when I was about three years old, my father came home once, and then he went back again to make some more money. He must have been going back and forth.

That's why my mother did the farming alone, and when they earned money, they'd buy fields. My parents' family was a so-called branch. When my father came to set up his own household, he must have received a share of the fields, but he didn't own a lot, so he went to do migrant work, I think. My mother was a hard worker, and even when she had somebody else come in and do the heavy work, she'd manage everything else in the house by herself. She was a neat, tidy person, and even her little fields, everybody said, looked smooth and clean like tatami floors.

There were four of us children, and I was the third. My father was never around when I was little. Even so, I never felt lonely. I remember being happy because when money came from Canada, I'd get things bought for me. The last time my father came home, he rebuilt the house. But it took more money than he expected, and there were other things he wanted to buy, and so he said he'd go off again and earn some more. The passport came through, but he started saying he didn't want to go that time. He stayed at home, farming. He died when he was about 60.

Thanks to my father doing that work overseas, I grew up without wanting anything. There was more than enough rice at home, and we always had enough to eat. We must have been average as a farm family. It was a poor village, but nobody was really down and out. I never heard of any talk about people selling their daughters. And very few girls left the village to work as domestics.

They had a primary school in the village, but it only went to the fourth grade, and beyond that you had to go to Hikone. We couldn't go back and forth that far, so I quit after the fourth grade. That's why I'm uneducated. There were only one or two children from the village every year who went on to the girls' high school in Hikone. In those days, studying wasn't as important for a girl as needlework. If you couldn't sew, you were shamed. I used to go to take lessons from a sewing teacher in Hikone.

I took lessons till I was past 20, and I got good enough to sew kimonos out of silk, double-lined crepe it was. I made all my wedding clothes myself. But even if I sewed clothes for somebody else, for practice, I didn't get paid. So I never earned money when I was a girl. When I was growing up, my family was raising silkworms, and it was terrible work to get the silk out, three times a year. I used to sew while I helped out with the housework, and I was almost never allowed to go out. I almost never went out of the village, either. If you went out, you had to be years older, and then it would be something like going to Kyoto to visit the head temple. Everybody in the village was Buddhist and there were a lot of temples. My parents and ancestors were all Pure Land Buddhists.

A lot of my classmates in primary school came to Canada later; they're all dead now. When we started getting older, we'd start wanting to go somewhere. Then, we'd hear people just back from "America," talking big. So we'd start thinking America was a wonderful place, and everybody would want to go. In our village, everybody wanted to go to America. My oldest sister was married and living in Vancouver. My second sister's husband went to Canada too, for a little while; he made a lot of money and came back. So I got wanting to go to America, too. To my way of thinking, it would be better than getting married to a farmer from the village.

I was around 22 when my sister in Vancouver got sick and came back to our house with her little girl. A year later, she died at home. Then, there was talk of my getting married to my brother-in-law to replace my sister. I didn't think that would be too bad; I wanted to go anyhow. Because all my friends were going, you see.

So we wrote to each other and got engaged, but as I was getting ready to leave, a strange thing happened. We found out that while my sister was sick and on her way home, my brother-in-law in Vancouver had found another woman. Seems she was a maid in his house. I mean, that woman herself wrote a letter about it to my parents. She was living in my sister's house, and she was pregnant, too. So the arrangements for me to marry my brother-in-law were cancelled.

But as my sister's little girl was in our house, my brother-in-law came back to our village for a visit. Then once again the talk of marriage came up. He was from the same village, and he was a distant relative. He said he wasn't with the woman who worked for him as a maid, and he talked to my parents till he finally got his way. I didn't have any leeway to say what I wanted, one way or the other. Anyhow, that was the cause of it. Things got arranged and I was married in my parents' house. I was to go to Vancouver with my niece, and my husband went ahead of us.

My husband's house was on Powell Street, right in the middle of the Japanese area of Vancouver. He had a grocery and a bathhouse to run, so he was pretty well off. My parents thought, he isn't a labourer but a businessman, so if he has a wife, she won't have to go out to work. It isn't a bad situation. My niece was six years old then, but my mother took her over for the time being, and I left her behind to go to Vancouver. I had all the new wedding things that my parents had bought for me, and I was wearing an old Western dress of my dead sister's. It must have been the year the First World War ended, 1918, I forget the name of the ship, but I came with a whole lot of other brides. I was 24.

When the boat got to Victoria, my husband wasn't even there to meet me. He'd sent somebody else, though. Since there was nothing I could do about it, I waited in a hotel, and he came along a few days later. No wonder he was late. When I got to the house in Vancouver, I found that woman living in the house, and she wouldn't leave. It seems my husband was embarrassed in front of the other relatives, but they'd had a child. That's how it came about he couldn't separate from her. I came officially as a wife with guarantees from a lot of cousins, but the woman just wouldn't leave the house. So what was the use of guarantees like that? I was the loser.

I stayed in that house for a month or two, but the woman made a fuss, saying she wouldn't leave him. That wasn't any pleasure. I got to feeling I didn't want to stay and I left. My parents said I wasn't to stay, and should come home. I had an aunt in Vancouver, so I got to stay with her until things were worked out. When I left my husband, everything was all right for him; he was with that woman. He was until he died. Afterwards I got to thinking my husband had never wanted to marry me at all, but at the time, I didn't understand.

My aunt said that if I stayed at home I'd start brooding, so she'd take me to a place where I could do housework. It was a missionary's house. He was a white man, but he could speak Japanese because he'd worked in Japan. So I could be of use to him. His Japanese was good, and he taught me a lot of things, but I'd just arrived, so I didn't know how to get along. My divorce wasn't settled, and I cried a lot. I worked there for about three months when I found I was pregnant. I had to have an operation for extrauterine pregnancy. I'd spent less than six months in Canada when I went back to Japan.

While I was working as a housekeeper, I met someone who wanted to marry me. My uncle was sympathetic and encouraged me, and made the arrangements. My husband-to-be was a fisherman and had his own boat, and I heard he'd become an owner-fisherman, with hired men. I kept company with him, but just for a very short time. He wasn't a bad person, I thought, but when it came time for me to go back to Japan for the operation, that was the end of the talk about marriage. But later, I was to get married to him.

I hurried back to Japan, and had an operation in a hospital in Kyoto. Thank goodness I got better. After the operation I went back to my parents, and then the man who was to be my second husband came to Japan and visited our house. My parents approved and things were arranged all at once. So before a year had gone by, I got married again in my parents' house. I must have thought I wanted to make a fresh start by getting married again. My husband was from Toyama Prefecture, and he had a very good character.

When we came back to Canada, it was the fishing season, and so we went and worked at a place on the Skeena. He caught salmon and I was a cook's helper at a cannery, and lived in at the cannery for the season. After getting married and living together, I noticed soon enough that my second husband was a very jealous man. All I had to do was talk to somebody and he'd get jealous. It got worse and worse. When we were working on the Skeena, a place with nothing but men, he got even more jealous.

When we married in Japan I thought he was an ordinary man, but you really don't know people until you start living with them. The people we worked with said that he probably got jealous because he cared so much for me, but I couldn't stand it. You see, he wanted me to stay at home all day long and not talk to anybody. So he didn't even give me spending money. He wasn't the type to get drunk and violent, he was just jealous. He was a strange one. He had to be sick. That kind of sickness lasts till you die. I grew up in the country, and didn't know there were people like that. I just spent one year with this man.

When the fishing was done, we went back to Vancouver; we were together for a while, but I didn't think I could stay with him much longer. So I had a friend take me away, and I went out doing day work, that is housework in the daytime. I went around to white people's houses and worked all day long to get just $1.50. Even at that, they gave me car fare and lunch, so it was a lot better than staying at home.

Then, my husband would come around to wherever I was working and follow me; he'd lie in wait. He'd eavesdrop on my conversations too, and I couldn't even talk to anyone. In the end he turned violent and it was terrible. Time and again I left home, and at last I couldn't stand it any more and I ran away to the shelter in Victoria. I went with only the clothes I had on me, and without a cent. It sounds like something out of a movie or a play, doesn't it?

The shelter was run by white missionaries, Methodists, and they took in people that were having trouble, and had nowhere to go. When I went, there were five Japanese women. They were all married and they all had problems. It's amazing how you meet people just like yourself in life. Some of them were in the same fix that I was. One was from Kumamoto, she was a midwife and did massage. She'd run away from a jealous husband too. When she went to bed, he'd tie a cord around her ankles so she couldn't get out of the room. She couldn't take it any more and ran away.

I got to come to this shelter because the white missionary I'd done housekeeping for happened to hear about me. He said there was this home for people in trouble, and arranged for me to go there. People like me without money, they let us stay for nothing. The missionary took me as far as the ferry to Victoria and even bought me a ticket, because I was just like naked, I had run away without bringing anything with me. They arranged for somebody to come to meet me in Victoria, and I really appreciated it. In this shelter, some Christians were working for Chinese and Japanese women in trouble, and there were a lot of orphans, too. There must have been about 40 people at that home.

If it hadn't been for the shelter, I don't think I could have become divorced. My husband would have suspected me of everything. He was crazy, and used to say I'd been friendly with other men. On top of that, he put me through some tough times. Even so, he asked me through a Japanese minister to come back. But the teacher at the home kept him from seeing me, and arranged for me to get a divorce. They were very nice and helped me out, the missionary and the teachers at the home.

The Japanese won't help you at all, even if you're down on your luck. I had a lot of rich relatives, but not a single one would lend me money. They were running businesses, and it wouldn't have been anything for them to put one or two people on the payroll, but not one of them invited me to stay with them. My mother sent me clothes and money, though, because she was worried.

The one person that helped me out from beginning to end was the missionary. I didn't know anything about Christianity, but I thought Christians were good people. When I was in the home, I studied the Christian religion a little with the teacher, so I became a Christian. Earlier in Vancouver, I just went to the temple, the Buddhist church, but I got baptized by the head pastor at the shelter in Victoria.

I was in the home for about six months, and little by little I started getting better. I was 26, but I got to feel I'd never go back to Japan again, and I was going to work no matter what. At the home, they'd choose only good Christian families to send us to do housework. We used to practice going outside, back and forth from the shelter, so we could get back into the world and start working again. At the house I worked in, the missus was very kind, and she taught me all kinds of cooking, like baking bread. I just spoke broken English, but she taught me things in a way I could understand, and I really learned from her.

I left the shelter to live in the house of some English people, and worked there about five years. The husband was a military man, a captain in the navy. The wife had died and there were four children, and a grandmother. They needed somebody who could do plain cooking. The work was easy and I got lots of money, $45 a month. That was a top wage for live-in housekeepers. I'd bake bread and make jam and marmalade, and they were happy, they said everything tasted good.

The father was a military man, so he had strict rules for the family. The children never came into the kitchen. They had set times to get up in the morning and go to bed at night, and those hours were always the same. That was the first time I saw children being brought up strictly, English style.

In five years, I'd saved up money because I hardly ever spent any, and I got to send a little to my mother back in Japan. But it seems my mother just put that money into the bank under my name. She thought I would come back to Japan some day, and she was thinking I would be able to live alone there.

I was around white people all the time, so I got to understand English well. The best way to learn English is to live in white people's houses. I hardly saw any Japanese, so I learned a lot. That was a good thing, but I couldn't do housework forever. In Victoria, there wasn't any other kind of work. At the time, sewing got to be popular among the Japanese, and I liked sewing, so I started thinking it would be better to learn dressmaking as a trade.

I left Victoria, where I'd lived for six years, and moved to Vancouver. There was a dressmaking school for Japanese only, run by a Mrs M., so that's where I went. They said three months would be enough, but I stayed for a whole year, learning.

At first, I was doing day work at the same time as I was going to dressmaking school, but I quit soon because I thought it would be better to do just one thing, and I was at school from morning to night, sewing. A friend of the teacher's had a dry-cleaning business, and I was told, he's looking for someone to mend dresses, so why don't you go and see about it. I spent about a year in his shop learning how to do mending and dry cleaning. I'd learned to speak English, so I could take care of the customers while I learned how to do business. And then, at last, I started wanting my own shop.

Just before the Depression, I think in 1927, I opened a business on Broadway, in a busy part of town. It was convenient for transportation, but the rent was really high. I paid $40 a month. It was on the street corner and both sides of the shop had windows, so it stood out; that made it a good place for business. I partitioned off the back, put in a kitchen and bed to make a room for myself, and I lived there. So, I managed with my broken English, and somehow, without asking anybody for help, I went to get my licence for the store. That was a dry cleaning shop I started off with.

In those days, everybody got a dry-cleaner's licence to do dressmaking. The washing, I sent out to somebody I knew, and I did the pressing myself. Then in my spare time, it was mainly mending and sewing women's clothes. I put up a sign "Fashion Dressmaking." All the money I'd saved up, I spent, and it was expensive to open the store. It was so long ago I don't remember how much it cost, but for sure, I managed by myself without borrowing.

Around then I brought over my younger brother from Japan, and that took money, so I went to my relatives to borrow some, but they wouldn't lend me any. They had money, but relatives are like that. I'd had the experience before, but from then on I decided I'd never go borrowing money from anybody again. In the ten years since coming to Canada, I'd had two setbacks, and in spite of that, I'd come to run my own business. I sent for my younger brother because he said he wanted to come to Canada. I was lonesome by myself, so if my brother was around, I'd cheer up. He said he wanted to come over for a while and make money, because he had three children and life was hard. He left his family behind to come here alone. He worked around New Westminster in the mountains and the sawmills, and worked about 20 years in Canada till he went home on account of the war. Those weren't very good times, and he had some real trouble over here too, so I helped him out as much as I could.

My shop was in a good location, so a lot of customers came in. When I was busy, I got Japanese housewives to come in and help out for low wages, but I'm the type to work by myself, and didn't hire people very much. I like to work away all alone. The customers were all white people. There were a lot of Salvation Army uniforms brought in. It was work with deadlines, so I had to finish by a certain time. A lot of nights, I worked till the sun came up. In Vancouver there were a lot of Japanese dressmakers, they say about 40 in those days, but not many like me, a woman working alone. Plenty of married women worked at home as dressmakers. The Japanese seem to be suited to dressmaking.

It was a business, but still it was manual work, and it was all I could manage just with my two hands. It was impossible to do things in a big way. I brought in three sewing machines and put motors in them. There were a lot of Japanese dry cleaners too, and they competed with each other. The men would do things up big; they'd buy new pressing machines, but I couldn't afford to, so I did everything the hard way, by hand. What you got for your labour was low, too. It was "two for one dollar," meaning if you cleaned two suits, you got a dollar; that was really cheap. The charge for sewing was low, too. A skirt cost $1.50, a dress $2 or $3, and a suit $6 or $7.

No matter how hard you tried, you were lucky if you could make two skirts a day, so you couldn't even make $4 a day. I'm not sure, but it seems I charged less than white dressmakers did. I never paid attention to the going rate. I was in business for nearly 20 years, but never raised my prices once. The rates were low, so the customers were glad to bring me their clothes. And on top of that, my work was neat, and I put everything into it. I wanted my customers to be happy. There were stories about people who earned a lot of money, but I know I didn't because it's in my nature to take too much trouble and I spent too much time on my work. I was the type who, if one stitch was crooked, I wanted to do it over again, so that wasn't good for business. I thought all I needed was enough money to live on.

But I think it's surprising I worked like that, and made my way. On Sundays, I used to close the shop and work inside, and never took any time off the whole year long. Day after day I sewed, and I worked without thinking it was a hardship. When summer came, I'd go down to the beach for a little while, but otherwise I hardly ever went out. And "going out" meant going to church every Sunday.

For a while too, I went to English school at night and learned speaking, reading and writing, enough to get along. Now I've forgotten everything, though. The United Church opened a night school for Issei, and taught English. I didn't have any trouble talking to my customers, but I didn't know grammar, so I spoke broken English. There must have been 80 of us at the school. I went about three years, but it made me busy just going to lessons, and there was no time for practice, so it didn't stick.

I used to hear there was a lot of discrimination in Vancouver, but that had nothing to do with me. I don't know why people don't like the Japanese. When I read the Japanese papers, they were always talking about people being anti-Japanese, but personally I didn't feel it one bit. Even when I was in business, I didn't feel any discrimination or prejudice. All my customers were nice, and not a single one would have discriminated. In 20 years there was only once when a customer wouldn't pay the bill, so practically all the white people were honest with me, too.

Even in the Depression, the customers never stopped coming. They came because my rates were low. It wasn't only that; it was because my work was so good that they were glad to bring in their orders. Competition shows if you're good or not. I never even wondered what kind of work my white competition was doing. I just thought it would be nice, if only my customers were happy, and I sincerely put everything into my work. That's why even in the middle of the Depression I was able to go on doing business and got enough to live on, and even had some money to spare.

In 1936, not long before the war, I took two months off and went to Japan. I'd been thinking about going back just once, because my mother was getting old. I took my brother, he hadn't been back for seven years, and paid for his expenses and pocket money and everything. This was the first pleasure trip in my life. On the boat, going and coming back, I had time to relax. I visited Kyoto and Nara, and went back home; I had to look as if I was doing my duty towards my mother. I remember she told us: "Just because you've gone to Canada doesn't mean you can climb the ladder in a hurry. When you're young you may think you can go up, but once you're older, you can't."

Somehow, I'd managed to stand on my own two feet and was confident I could make my way in life, and I wanted to put my mother's mind at ease. But just like a parent, she was terribly worried. She'd bought a few fields in my name so I'd be able to get along alone, even if I came back to Japan. That land got taken away in wartime because the farmlands were "freed" and they said I was an absentee landlord, but you really feel grateful to parents, don't you? My mother thought I was all alone because of my unhappy marriages, so I'd come back some day. In the meanwhile war broke out and I couldn't go back to Japan, but my mother was waiting for me. My brother left Canada during the war and took his place in the family. My mother retired and she waited for me to come back. In 1953 she died; she was nearly 90.

When the war came, I worried, wondering if I'd be able to stay in business, but there was nothing I could do. I didn't read the newspapers much, so I didn't know any facts in detail. There was nothing to do. We were told to leave Vancouver, and I went to a ghost town, Slocan. I held out until the very end, it must have been October 1942, and I left Vancouver on the last train to the ghost towns. I didn't want to leave, but what was the use, Japan was at war, and I wasn't especially angry. I wasn't naturalized, so if they called me an enemy alien, I couldn't do anything.

My landlord, who lived on the second floor up from my store, was angry saying Japan had made a sneak attack on Pearl Harbor, but he didn't tell me to get out. He let me know that he'd come and help me if I needed him, so I should just yell for him. That was because a lot of times, people would come and make trouble in the middle of the night, throwing stones and yelling "Jap, Jap." If you take them one at a time, though, white people are all pretty nice. The customers kept coming in with their orders as usual.

Now, I stayed in Slocan for nearly three years, thinking what a bore it was. I didn't have any children to take care of, and my work was, I got up in the morning and ate breakfast; I ate three meals a day, taking my time, and for the rest I loafed around. I got welfare from the government and lived on $25 a month. If you get welfare, you can't work. Once I taught dressmaking in secret, but somebody reported me to the government, so that came to an end.

The Japanese were mean to each other; they'd fight, and it was very unpleasant. Even when we got shut away, I didn't get mad at the government at all. I don't know how often I got angry, more at the trouble among the Japanese than at the government. So from early on, I wanted to move east, I waited to get out. I thought that anywhere I went, as long as I had a job, things would work out. I was confident I could make a living as long as I could sew. It wouldn't be any use going back to Japan, because I wasn't likely to find any work there. I had no trouble deciding what to do, when I thought I'd like to move east. Before the government said they'd send anybody that applied back to Japan, I'd come to Toronto.

I spent three years in the camp, but don't think it was all that useless. I got years living off the government, and got protected, so I felt that was all right. What I couldn't stand was the loafing around and the fighting every day, and that's why I wanted to go east early. Some people used to fill in the time going to plays or socials, but I'm not the going-out type, so I was bored, and couldn't help getting into silly arguments. It would have been all right if I'd started sewing classes and made some money, but in the camp, nobody could afford to make new dresses. They didn't have the means, so they couldn't do anything. Anyway I got a lot of free time in the camp. I was close to 50 years old, those are the best days of your working life. Well, maybe you can say I did waste my time there.

But going east, I didn't know what to expect. I meant to go into business, so I thought Toronto would be good and I applied to the Commission early. Somebody I knew came to Toronto before me, and offered to rent me a room. In March, the year the war ended, I came to Toronto with two sewing machines. Since my address was known, and I was trained to do something, the Commission approved. I had a train ticket bought for me, and I came with all the baggage I could bring. The house my friend had rented was right in the middle of the Jewish market, where Kensington Market is now. It was a very dirty place and I didn't think I could stand to stay there long, but I was glad just to have a room to stay in. The only people who would rent to Japanese were the Jews. Because the white people, it was the first time they'd seen Japanese, so they didn't know what we were like. They were afraid and wouldn't rent to us. It was really bad from the time I got there in March until August when the war ended.

I'd been idle for a whole three years, so I wanted to start working again as soon as possible. The morning after getting here I went out looking for work. Around Queen and Spadina, there were a lot of garment factories, and if you walked around looking, you could get work right away. My first job was only two days, but I remember it was sewing buttons on men's clothes. I'd been looking at a sign advertising for help, when the boss came outside and told me to start work right away. That was a Jewish factory, too.

The third day, I heard they were looking for help at Holt Renfrew on Yonge Street, that was the best women's clothing store in Toronto, so I went to apply. The personnel manager said "Don't you know there's a war on?" and I said "I know, but the war doesn't have anything to do with me. All I want is a job," but they wouldn't hire me. I kept insisting, and at last the boss phoned and sent for me, and said he'd hire anybody, any nationality, as long as they wanted to work. He gave me a job right away, mending dresses. This boss was Jewish, too.

I found out afterwards, that some people working there were prejudiced against Japanese. There were 15 of them, mostly English people. They did end up being nice to me, but at first, I was the only Japanese, and I couldn't work there and hold my head high. I got $18 a week and a cheque for $25 at Christmas. I was happy because I'd received such good money, only two or three days after coming to Toronto.

I got praised for doing neat work, but it was a big store, and they wouldn't raise the wages. Even after I'd been working two or three years, I didn't get a single dollar more. People said $18 was too low, so I left and worked in all kinds of factories, a good five years, maybe. At garment factories it was usually piecework, that is, a set wage for one item. It was tough work, and if you didn't work fast and finish a lot of pieces, you couldn't make money. I'm a slow worker, not suited to factory work. No matter how hard I worked, I didn't earn much. I earned a little more money than at Holt's but everybody competed in this work. It's awful to make money by piecework. It brings out too much stress in people. It was dreadful; it wasn't suited to me anyhow.

At Holt's and the factories too, the people I worked with were all immigrants: English, Scottish, Italian, Jewish, and they all competed with each other. At Christmas we had a party and we were all invited to a meal, but usually we didn't see each other outside of work. We didn't invite each other home, or go out together. My English was a lot better than it is now, so it was no problem talking to them. The Italians got along with their broken English too. All we did was work, say hello and goodbye and that was it. I didn't make friends with any of them.

I'd been living in rented rooms that I heard about from other Japanese, but after about 10 years in Toronto, I bought this house

I'm living in now. I put together all the savings I brought from Vancouver, and the insurance that matured, and I made the down payment, but it was hard. It must have been $8,000 and I spent the money I'd been saving from all those years working. I made the mortgage payments a little at a time every month, and about 10 years ago it was all paid for. Right after I bought it, I got two boarders, bachelors from my village in Shiga, so I finally settled down in my own place. Before that, I'd always been a renter, and I had wanted my own house. For a while, I used to look after the boarders; I cooked for them, but that was hard so I decided to do dressmaking at home, and quit my job.

I hung a dressmaker's sign outside the house and started business. I was really busy, even in a place like this. The house wasn't built like a store, but it was on a bus route so people would see the sign and come in. That's the work I did till I turned 70 and started getting my pension.

Some Japanese live around here, but mixed in with a lot of other nationalities. So even if there's some people prejudiced against Japanese in particular, they don't stand out. There's a lot of prejudice against Italians, too. The Japanese have a name for them. It isn't just the Japanese, all the races are prejudiced against each other.

I had a lot of trouble with my Jewish customers and even had fights with them. They were always the ones who complained after their dresses were finished. They'd say the dress was no good here, they didn't care for it there. And it was only the Jews who asked for a deal on my rates. They gave me so much trouble, I ended up not taking any more Jewish customers. If they came, I told them I was busy.

My younger brother, the one who went back to Japan during the war, died in 1964 and his family said they had trouble making ends meet. So every month for five years I sent them money. Not that they asked for it, but I'd get letters saying, thanks to your money, the family he left behind gets enough to eat, so I couldn't very well not send them money. In the end, I must have sent tens of thousands of dollars. My brother was pretty unlucky. Just after he went back to Japan his wife died, and he was left with the children and it seems he had a bad time of it.

When the war began he got sent to a road camp in B.C. and stayed there for a while, but when the repatriation boats were going out, he started wanting to go back to Japan. When I was in Slocan he came visiting, and I tried to persuade him to stay in Canada. But he said he'd left his family behind in Japan, so it was better for him to go back while the government was offering him the chance. I sent him off with a lot of things, as I thought people would be in trouble in Japan, and I gave him some money, too. He got remarried and had a child, but he couldn't feed a family just by working. He did things like selling off land, and he wasn't making a very good living. Then after a struggle he died too, and his family was even worse off. So no matter what happened I had to help them out, didn't I?

I sent for a child of his, thinking we'd live together. I spent a lot of money, and went around asking for help, and finally adopted her, but right away she went and got married. She favoured her husband, and fell out with me, so we weren't together for long. She said she couldn't live with me very easily, so she left, and I lost out. I didn't have any more to do with that girl.

In 1969 I went back to Japan for the first time. I meant to stay for a good long time, a year or so, but my brother had died, and there was a new generation of relatives, so things were completely different in my family. The fields, all the property, belonged to my brother's second wife now. The fields that my mother had gradually bought up for me, the government had taken them away. I went to the courts, but nothing came of it. I'd thought I'd come back to Japan when I was old and live on my pension from Canada. That's what I was hoping. If only I had land, I could live alone, I thought. If only I had money I could go back to Japan to live. But I was wrong to think so. At my family's house, it was all in-laws, and the feeling was completely different, so it wasn't the country that I used to know.

I'd become a Canadian citizen, but kept my Japanese citizenship too. Even after 60 years in Canada, I didn't know English well, so you can't say I've become a Canadian. When you get old, you're out of touch with the world, so even in this country, I'm a Canadian in name only. It's getting further and further away. At elections, I vote, but don't know who to choose. If you ask around, everybody has a different opinion. I just decide by myself; it depends on my mood.

I've lost touch with things in Japan too, but I'm always thinking of my home town. I want to see it again. My family's grave and my own grave are over there. If I go back to Japan and things work out all right, then I'll live there; if not, I'll come back and live in Canada. But that may be too late. Every day I think I'll go and see, but I can't travel alone. And there's nobody asking me to come back.

I don't have any children, so I half feel I want to stay in this country, and I half feel I want to go back to Japan. I don't care to die in this country. I haven't been lucky with my family, so there's nothing to be done about it, is there? When I was young I had any number of proposals to get married again. In Vancouver, there weren't enough women to go around, so lots of men were proposing. I had very bad luck twice, I couldn't stand it. After that I turned everybody down, but sometimes I think it would have been nice to have a child. But it's too late now.

Both my husbands had money, and I was the real wife, but I didn't take a penny from either of them. But I was the one who put out the money, and I didn't take any at all; I left it behind me. I wasn't driven out, so that's the way it had to be. If you're talking about money, I saved it up by working hard. That was the only kind I ever earned. And if you talk about dressmaking rates, if I'd charged as much as other people, the money would have piled up and I wouldn't have looked like a fool. I thought it would be all right to earn just enough to live on, and I worked without thinking about making any more. I wonder what I've worked for. I don't understand, myself.

The future Mrs Nakamura (left) and family, Hiroshima, Japan, 1910s.
Nakamura Family Collection, Montreal, Que.

Early Japanese settlers at a logging camp near Woodfire, B.C., n.d.
Japanese Canadian Cultural Centre, Toronto, Ont.

Married couple, 1910s. Kutsukake Family Collection, Toronto, Ont.

Newly married immigrant couple, Vancouver, B. C., 1910s. Kutsukake Family Collection, Toronto, Ont.

A Japanese family—the early years, n.p., 1915. Japanese Canadian Cultural Centre, Toronto, Ont.

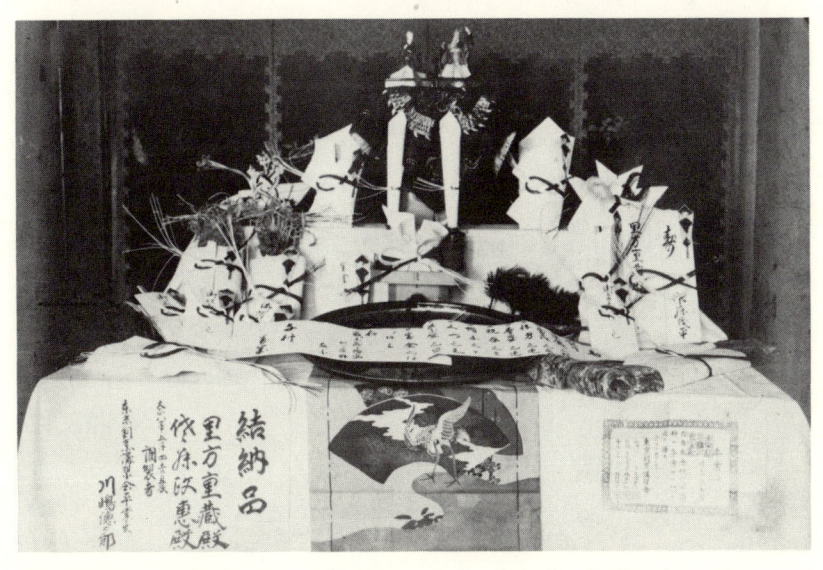

Betrothal presents, n.p., 1919. Kutsukake Family Collection, Toronto, Ont.

Immigrant family, Vancouver, B.C., 1920s. Kutsukake Family Collection, Toronto, Ont.

Japanese women in Vancouver, B.C., 1920s. Japanese Canadian Cultural Centre, Toronto, Ont.

The teacher and students of a sewing class held in a dress-making shop, Vancouver, B.C., 1920s. Kutsukake Family Collection, Toronto, Ont.

Mr Kaburagi's English class, Vancouver, B.C.(?), 1920s. Japanese Canadian Cultural Centre, Toronto, Ont.

Japanese children taking part in a July 1st festival parade, Vancouver, B.C., n.d. Kutsukake Family Collection, Toronto, Ont.

Mrs and Mr Hayashi and son with Edward, Prince of Wales, near High River, Alta., 1920s. Japanese Canadian Cultural Centre, Toronto, Ont.

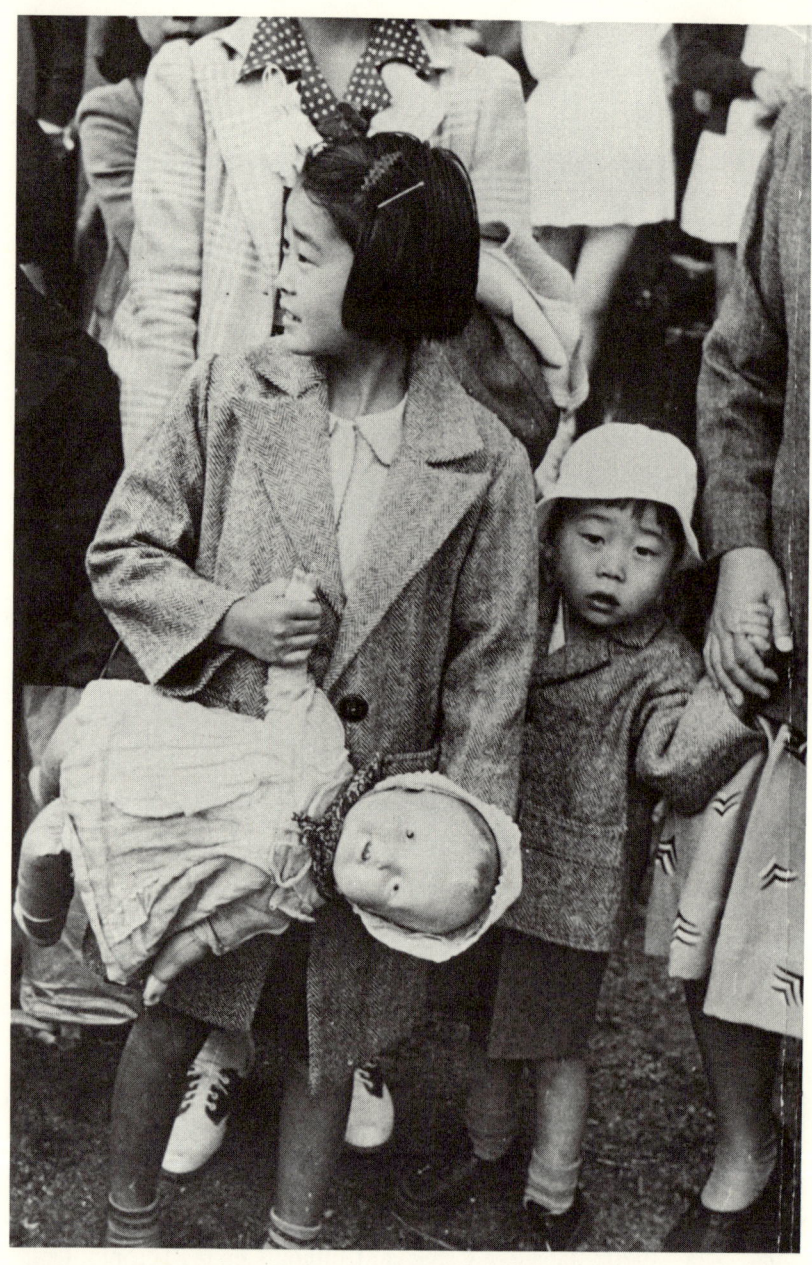

Children waiting to be evacuated to the internment camps, Vancouver, B.C., February 1942. Japanese Canadian Cultural Centre, Toronto, Ont.

Needlework class at Greenwood Internment Camp, B.C., July 1945.
Japanese Canadian Cultural Centre, Toronto, Ont.

Japanese evacuees from British Columbia harvest sugar beets, Alberta, 1944. Japanese Canadian Cultural Centre, Toronto, Ont.

Repatriates leaving Slocan, B.C., for Japan, 1946. Japanese Canadian Cultural Centre, Toronto, Ont.

When my husband and I got together, people criticized. Even the newspapers ...

Mrs Yasu Ishikawa

4 Mrs Yasu Ishikawa

The central figures in this chapter and the next, Mrs Yasu Ishikawa and Mrs Tami Nakamura, both come from Hiroshima Prefecture. With its neighbour, Yamaguchi Prefecture, Hiroshima was known before the war as a major source of emigration among Japanese prefectures. The Inland Sea region, which straddles the boundary between these two prefectures, was especially prominent from the beginning of the government-contract labour system in 1885 until World War II.

The people in the region from the Bay of Hiroshima to the Inland Sea had enjoyed a close relationship with the sea since early times, and they had many occasions to go to far-off places and learn about the outside world. It seems that a number of fishermen went as far away as the island of Tsushima, between Kyushu and Korea.

From early times, fishing boats and fishermen had been more active here than elsewhere, and it was also a culturally advanced area. As I rode on a slow train on the former Sanyo Railway line which runs along the coast of the Inland Sea, where the sun shone brightly, I thought there was something in the geography and the climate of the region which made its people liberated and active.

In Hiroshima Prefecture, if you leave the coast and make for the interior, the climate and scenery change completely as you approach the Chugoku mountain range. Mrs Yasu Ishikawa's home village, Yuki-cho in the district of Jinseki, is located in a mountain area. If you get off at Shin'ichi Station on the Fukushio Line, about halfway between the cities of Fukuyama and Miyoshi, you are at the entrance to Yuki-cho. From this area, you see nothing but mountains. The temperature drops by several degrees, and the atmosphere is completely different from that of the coast. It is somewhat reminiscent the Tohoku area where I come from. You have a sense of being shut in, enclosed by mountains.

It is, therefore, not surprising to hear Mrs Ishikawa say, "There was almost no overseas emigration from the Yuki-cho area," even though it is in Hiroshima Prefecture. One reason is probably the climate and natural features of the area.

Mrs Ishikawa, who had the "weird ambition" of wanting to go overseas to a place where nobody from the village of Yuki had ever gone, has most certainly led an exceptional life. The parts of Hiroshima which had produced a great number of emigrants were limited to very specific regions, as in the case of Shiga and Yamaguchi Prefectures, and almost nobody left from Jinseki-gun. If the village people, let alone her relatives, did not speak well of Mrs Ishikawa's ambition, it was because she had no predecessors.

The most prominent areas of overseas emigration from Hiroshima were the towns and villages on the western coast of the prefecture, and those of the plains in the valley of the Ota River lying in the direction of the city of Hiroshima. In these areas the "America Village" phenomenon could be seen. Since at peak periods, almost 30 per cent of the population of villages, such as Nihota, Kuchida, and Jigozen, went overseas, the centres are well known as subjects of surveys by both geographers and historians.[1]

According to *The History of Hiroshima Prefecture*, the economic structure of prominent emigration areas differed from that of other regions for the following reasons:

1. The population density was much higher than the prefectural average.
2. Each farm household had a much smaller area of cultivation than the prefectural average.

---

[1] 1 Tomoki Ishikawa, "Hiroshima-wanganchi Gozenmura keiyaku imin no shakai chirigakuteki kosatsu" ("Socio-geographical study of contract emigration from Gozen Village on the coast of Hiroshima Bay"), *Jinbin Chiri (Human Geography)*, vol. 19, No. 1, 1967.

———, "Hiroshima-ken Nanbu Kuchita-mura keiyaku imin no shakai chirigakuteki kosatsu" ("Socio-geographical study of contract emigration from Kuchita Village in southern Hiroshima Prefecture"), *Shigaku kenkyu (Historical Studies)*, No. 99, 1967.

———, "Setonai chiiki kara no imin" ("Emigration from the Inland Sea area"), *Shigaku kenkyu (Historical Studies)*, No. 126, 1975.

3. The rate of cultivated-land use was high, and there was more intensive farming than elsewhere; the harvest per unit of rice field was higher than the prefectural average.
4. Commodity crops, such as cotton, rushes, and indigo were widespread, especially cotton cultivation which was labour intensive.
5. Landlord and tenant relationships were well evolved, but the proportion of independent landed farmers was also high: these were areas of intermediate progress in development.[2]

In "areas of intermediate development," the number of landed farmers began to decline from the middle of the Meiji Period, while that of tenant farming increased. Evidently the farming class was breaking up at a rapid rate. In the process of dissolution, the main household of a family often weakened, and the cadet families became independent. In that case, there was probably little opposition to young men cutting themselves free of the conservatism of the villages and going elsewhere in Japan, or even abroad. With the Meiji Period, emigration to Hawaii and North America began. The ever-increasing population and the excess labour could only be absorbed by migrant work abroad. The idea was enormously attractive.

The fact that the emigrants included many heads of households and first sons[3] can be explained simply through the phenomenon of migrant work. However, it may also have been a result of an advance in the process of the breakup of the family, which had been the base of agricultural society. Away from the bonds of family, individuals could act with relative freedom. There were also a number of factors which enabled the villagers to not view emigration as a tragic escape. The regions of Hiroshima Prefecture most notable for emigration may not have been alone in being particularly developed areas. It would appear that, in general, the conditions which favoured emigration existed in the social structure of southwest Japan rather than the northwest.

---

[2] *Hiroshima-ken shi* (*History of Hiroshima*), "Kindai I "Kaigai e no imin" ("Modern Period I: Overseas Emigration"), Hiroshima Prefecture, 1980.

[3] Op. cit., Ishikawa.

The question of origins aside, the social phenomenon called overseas emigration began and continued in certain regions because the bonds between the parent village and the people abroad consisted almost exclusively of blood ties and territorial relationships. An individual such as Mrs Ishikawa, living in a small village in the district of Jinseki—even if it was in Hiroshima Prefecture—would not have heard people discussing emigration, and no information from other sources would have reached her. In those days, it was extremely difficult to go overseas without an intermediary. By Mrs Ishikawa's time, there was no way of emigrating to Canada unless someone already there sent for an individual. Since Mrs Ishikawa lacked connections, it seems that she consented to marriage to an outsider—though a native of the prefecture—whose background was not clearly known, because she was grateful to be "sent for."

In the case of Mrs Tami Nakamura, a resident of the city of Hiroshima, she was not preceded by a relative or anyone connected with the family. Evidently she grew up listening to talk about emigration which was on the level of rumour. She remembers that the first group of government-contract emigrants had already gone to Hawaii from the Nihota and Kusatsu areas outside the city, and that from the city, too, several hundred emigrants had left every year. There were also many companies actively operating as emigration agents, so that emigration must have been relatively common. Once it became known that a certain young woman wanted to go to America, marriage talks would spread by word of mouth. Mrs Nakamura thought she would prefer to go alone, rather than as a bride, so when she settled in Canada, she brought over her unmarried brother and sister. In the Nakamura family, they continued to send for people annually to the legal limit. In the end, they had taken more than 10 Japanese immigrants under their wing. All of them came from her husband's native place, Eba Ward in Hiroshima City.

Therefore, before World War II, there were almost no cases of emigrating alone without overseas relations. First, someone would go abroad, then he would send for his wife, children, then brothers and sisters, who might in turn send for others, so that the network spread. Those who entered its scope were blood relatives or fellow villagers. Family and territorial bonds were very important to the movements of population called overseas emigration, and to regional society. They also strongly contrast to the way I entered Canada as a postwar immigrant. I arrived here alone, without knowing anyone, and became an immigrant without anyone's help.

The movement of immigrants of the prewar type, dominated as it was by family and territorial bonds, had the natural result of influencing the way the Issei related to their new society. The Japanese immigrants transplanted, root and stock, the human relationships they were used to in their village societies to this new society, Canada. They placed a high value on blood relationships, and relied on their fellow villagers, centring their social life on them. This relationship was how Japanese villages that crossed the sea continued their existence in Canada.

For Hiroshima Prefecture, the peak period for emigration, from 1897 to the Gentlemen's Agreement of 1908, was the age of "free emigration." Almost all cases of emigration to Canada belonged to this type, except for women who were sent for as brides. Free immigration differed from the government-sponsored and the contract type, in that all expenses for passage were borne by the individual. When Mrs Nakamura's husband entered Canada, it was 1908, just when the Gentlemen's Agreement had been made, and Mr Nakamura represents a rare case of immigration without having been sent for. It appears that on his departure, he had prepared capital in the amount of 100 yen, roughly equivalent to 100 dollars at the time. This proved barely sufficient to cover expenses up to his arrival in Hawaii, so he worked in Hawaii for six months to raise money to go to Canada.

How much did it take for Mrs Nakamura to come to Canada as a bride, 10 years later? In the case of a picture bride, it was customary for the husband to bear the entire cost, and to send the money to Japan. It must have been a sort of engagement gift. Many people say they have no accurate memory of the amounts the bride's family received. Apparently, some men sent at least 100 or 200 yen, including money for preparations, so that the amount can be estimated at an average of 150 yen.

According to the materials in the *History of Hiroshima Prefecture*, it cost about 100 yen in 1906 to cross the Pacific, including the train from Hiroshima Station to Yokohama and then the boat to Hawaii. At the time, the monthly income of a carpenter was five or six yen, and the wholesale price of five bushels of unpolished rice was 40 yen. Therefore the expenses for going abroad were equivalent to two years of a carpenter's income, or the cost of 12.5 bushels of unpolished rice.

Those people who wished to emigrate were forced to sell their fields or borrow money from acquaintances, relatives, or people of means in the village on the condition that they would settle their debts after they got established abroad or on their return to Japan. For example, there seems to have been a custom in the village of Toita in Aki-gun, Hiroshima Prefecture, for a man of means to advance some capital to an aspiring migrant worker without travel money, who would then repay the sum through remittances from overseas.[4]

At any rate, one can say that the road to overseas emigration was closed to people who were unable to raise funds. Individuals who were able to supply a minimum of some 100 yen were generally of the middle to upper strata of the agricultural class, including a number of landowners. The mutual aid associations in the villages may have been a factor, but not all villagers had access to these organizations: their use was probably limited to those with a certain position and capital.

Then, even if these individuals borrowed in order to get to Canada, they found it was impossible to make money. They were unable to save or to make remittances. It was a struggle to save the money needed to get married. Mrs Yasu Ishikawa's husband was 35 when he married, and "a man who was so incapable that all he sent me was 60 yen for the passage." It was only later, when Mrs Ishikawa herself lived and worked in Canada, that she realized if you made under two dollars a day, you barely survived, and it was difficult to send a remittance of even 100 dollars.

Spadina Avenue in Toronto, where the Ishikawas live, is the equivalent of Asakusa in Tokyo. It has a working class atmosphere, distinctive even compared to other working class areas in the city. Spadina Avenue is the street where I walked the most frequently in my student days, and I often dropped in on the Ishikawas to have a cup of tea. After a 10-minute trip from the university library, Spadina turns into Chinatown. There are about 30 Chinese restaurants on this street, offering inexpensive meals of rice or noodles, which satisfy the large appetites of poor students. I owe a great debt to Chinese restaurants. Had it not been for Spadina Avenue, I would not have had a student life.

Spadina, a student neighbourhood, is also an immigrant district. Half of the millions of people who entered Canada during the post World War II immigrant boom aimed for Ontario, especially Toronto, as their place of permanent residence. People from all over the world came to Toronto, and perhaps most of them have walked down Spadina Avenue at least once. Among them were the Ishikawas, who moved to Toronto after the war and bought the house where they are living now.

The Ishikawa house is a three-storey brick structure built a century

---

[4] Op. cit., *Hiroshima-ken shi*.

ago, and is located in the midsection of Spadina Avenue. For a time, Mrs Ishikawa ran a coffee shop a little way down from this house. The Ishikawas are probably among the few residents who have observed so many changes in the neighbourhood after the war, the many comings and goings of immigrants. Mr Ishikawa is fond of the area, so open and full of life, and even nowadays, when he is nearing 90, he never fails to take regular walks. He says the feel of the street air on his skin keeps him from aging.

Mrs Ishikawa is now in complete retirement, so she is spending all her days in comfort. She says she realizes how the forgetfulness of old age worsens day by day. Her words do not come out immediately, and even when they do, they are full of mistakes, so that she complains she can no longer speak easily any more. She feels sad because even if she is materially well off, her health is not what it used to be. She feels sad. The opposite of her extroverted husband, she tends to keep her feelings to herself. These days, her only contact with the outside world is the weekly church service. Reading the books sent to her from Japan, and writing letters, she considers to be work.

Ever since her retirement, Mrs Ishikawa has been a member of an Issei haiku club, and is studying haiku composition. One of her recent poems goes "I've turned on the air conditioner—and here's a chair for old age, just right for reading," and she says, "I indulge myself a lot, and I don't want for anything." She is frugal by nature, though, and says she is as dead set against extravagance as she has ever been.

The furniture and other household effects are simplicity itself, and the only conspicuous item is a big colour TV, with the recent addition of a video machine. But the most luxurious item in the living room is a hanging scroll with calligraphy in the hand of the famous Christian Toyohiko Kagawa: "For God so loved the world that He gave His only begotten son," a sign of Mrs Ishikawa's religious faith, which goes far deeper than "mere praying."

To me, Mrs Ishikawa is rare among Issei women in that she came to Canada with a dream of becoming independent in life. She says that rather than come as a mere bride, she would have preferred to work, using the skills acquired in her training as a midwife. Apparently she came with a very strong desire for economic independence as a midwife "making big money" and for social recognition, "giving the job all I had, because I thought it was work that helped other people." After abandoning her career for marriage, she concentrated on being a helpmate, but it seems that she always made great efforts in order not to end up being a simple labourer.

That is why, I think, the narrowness of Japanese Canadian society sometimes made her very angry.

Mrs Ishikawa has no memory of experiencing discrimination or prejudice on the part of "Canadians"—meaning non-Japanese—but she has a profound distaste for the tiny world of the Japanese settlement. She criticizes her fellows harshly, saying that if they had looked at the outside world with an open mind, they would have made more money and not been so severely discriminated against. I was attracted by the fierce spirit and the critical attitude of this quiet, reticent woman, and I frequently went visiting to listen to her talk.

With the passing of time, the struggles of years gone by seem so vain in retrospect. Who has never felt this way in the process of aging? Mrs Ishikawa says that she frequently turns this thought over in her mind. Her husband, who was born brimming over with optimism and curiosity, and who is also a very upright person morally, takes immense pleasure in recalling days past. He is a fortunate man who can say firmly "I've done everything I ever wanted to do. I have no regrets at all." Thus the Ishikawas, in their individual ways, are living out their last years in comfortable tranquillity.

I was born and raised in the village of Yuki, Jinseki-gun in Hiroshima Prefecture. It was 1896 that I was born. Yuki is about 20 miles from Fukuyama, and it isn't very far from the city of Hiroshima, either. There was a subprefectural office in Yuki, and for a village, it was quite a good size. The primary school had an advanced course, and pupils from other villages nearby used to go to it.

My family was in trade, selling Japanese-style clothes. The third generation from my father's time is in the same business. It was a big family; I had eleven brothers and sisters, and I was the fifth, right in the middle, so I grew up getting jostled around. With all of us, plus the boys working in the store, we looked like a row of little statues at the temple.

My mother was always mending old clothes to dress us in, one after the other. I grew up in nothing but hand-me-downs from my older sisters. The girls in my family weren't allowed to work in the store. We were always in the back rooms, sewing or something. It was a small town, but we were in business, so every day a little money came in. We never had trouble making ends meet. Until the age of 20, I grew up without wanting for anything.

Around that time in Hiroshima, there were still *buraku*, villages for the lowest caste of people, and I remember some of these "new commoners" living on the outskirts of Yuki. They often came to our house to sell straw sandals. My family would buy ten, twenty of them at a time. My mother was the daughter of the household, and she was a generous person, the type to buy whatever she was asked to, sandals or anything else.

We were taught that these "new commoners" belonged to a different class of people. The food in their houses was supposed to be unclean, so we didn't eat it, that was the custom. Even when you were invited for a special celebration, you'd just sit with the meal in front of you, and nobody would eat. They knew this, so it seems they'd put some money in the bowls. Instead of having a feast, you'd go home with the money. We didn't care. But now, those people's children and grandchildren, they've all come up in the world. When I went back, they'd done so well for themselves it was amazing. They've even come to be village councillors and members of the National Assembly. Even in those days they all had some money. Probably, they put up with everything because they were discriminated against, and didn't spend their money. It's the same as the Japanese in Canada. We were discriminated against, so we struggled to do our best.

I graduated from the upper primary school course and went to supplementary classes for a year. When I was a child, I intended to go to "medical school." My brothers and sisters all did well in school, so I thought I could go, too. But my marks were just average, so I couldn't go on studying, and there was no "medical school" for me. My older sister had gone to Osaka and was working as a midwife, so I thought that would be a good idea. I got to spend two years at a school for midwives in Osaka and got some practical training as well, and I worked in my home town till I came over here.

As you see, I'm not good-looking, and even among my brothers and sisters I'm the plainest. That's why there was no talk of marriage for me even when I came of age. At the time, every girl got married by the age of 20. I thought that with my looks, nobody would ever marry me in Japan, and that I'd better go overseas. So I came after making up my own mind. I wanted to work very hard and make money. I thought, I can do it if I go to Canada, maybe, and work as a midwife. I hoped to make money, even enough to start up a bank with.

I had a lot of brothers and sisters and they'd all tease me for my plain looks. I've never forgotten that. I thought, darn it, if you're going to give me a hard time, I'll make a lot of money, I'll get rich, I'll show you. That's why I wanted to go to America and make a living for myself. Nowadays I've become shy, but when I was young, I had lots of spirit.

Hiroshima Prefecture sent out a lot of emigrants overseas, and it seems some came from Fukuyama, but I was the pioneer from Yuki. There was nobody before me who came to Canada, and nobody after. It was an unusual thing to do. When it was settled that I was going, everybody was amazed. Nowadays, people envy anybody going abroad, but in the old days, they really talked against you. I certainly had a hard time. I don't know how often my sister-in-law tried to talk me out of it. She said I shouldn't go to a place where I'd be without kith or kin, and I can't forget how hard she tried to keep me from going. I can still hear her voice. A lot of my relatives lived in town, and they were all against the idea.

Even if I wanted to be a midwife in Canada, it was impossible to go alone. That's why I got married. A friend in the village talked about a man, he was from Hiroshima too, that was looking for a wife, and I jumped at the idea. I got married without meeting the man. Since it was that kind of marriage, I suffered.

If you just looked at the pictures, he seemed to be a fine man, but he had no spirit. You don't really know people unless you've been seeing them for a while. The go-between only said nice things about him. It was true he liked to read novels, and he owned a lot of them, as the go-between said, but he didn't have anything between his ears. All the books he had were worthless. And he didn't have any ambition like the real workers who came over, meaning to earn money and go back. I put up with him for a year, though.

I had no idea what kind of person I had married, and what kind of life he was leading. Anyway, I had my heart set on coming here, and that was all I could think of. That was my dream, and I thought things would turn out all right. I was just a child, you see. There was no time for studying about Canada. I didn't even know what it meant not to know English. I thought I could get along with Japanese. Because I was young, all I could think of was coming here.

My father was dead set against the idea. "It's the most important thing in a lifetime, and anybody who wants to marry you should come in person. He can't be a suitable man, if he asks somebody else to look for a wife." My father turned out to be absolutely right. My mother was different, she told me to do what I thought was best. You're really grateful for parents. In the end, my father gave in, feeling he wanted to let his daughter do what she wanted. That's why I never went back to Japan, until the children were grown. I came here against people's objections, so I couldn't go back until I became self-supporting myself. I couldn't go back while my parents were alive.

I encouraged the marriage discussions with this man and entered his family register, and in summer of 1919 I came to Canada. I was 22 years old. I knew that my husband was a section chief on railway construction for the Canadian Pacific, but he probably didn't have much money. He'd sent me just enough for travel expenses, it must have been $60. All this money got returned when we separated later on; at the time, my parents gave me some spending money.

That was a time when a lot of brides were coming over, and we drew lots to decide who would leave first. I waited at an inn in Kobe. My parents came to Kobe and saw me off, crying all the time. I disobeyed my parents, and maybe that's why I was punished later on.

As I'd been learning how to play the lute, the *chikuzen biwa*, I brought my lute with me. When I arrived, I found there was simply no time to play it and its crepe silk cover ended up getting eaten by insects. I came on a Japanese mail boat named the *Kashima-maru*, and when we saw Victoria, I thought, what a beautiful place this is. When we landed, I was terribly nervous, wondering what kind of man would come and meet me.

He was good-looking, just like his pictures. But he didn't have any brains at all. I was very sad; there was a lump in my throat. We met, and right away I got depressed, wondering how on earth I was going to spend a whole lifetime with him. He was quite a bit older than me, too, but he had absolutely no spirit. And he wasn't smart. We didn't have anything in common to talk about. He was working on the railway, but he didn't earn much.

I could have put up with an ordinary man, but really, this one was below average. It was really trying, because there was nobody I could talk to about it. I'll never forget that feeling.

I was in that photo marriage for about a year. As I didn't have any feelings for him, he must have given up, too. After we separated, it took a year and a half to get my name taken off his family register, and not long after that, he died. While I was with him, all I did was write letters home every day. I apologized, saying everything had turned out the way my father had said, and that I had been wrong. He answered "Don't send any more letters like that. You're in the place you wanted to go to, so don't make any apologies"; he was angry. Other people said nasty things about me, too. It was all the more reason I felt it would be better to die, but then I thought, why should I die? I'll keep on living, and do all I can to show the whole world what I'm really like. What else can I do? I didn't feel like going back to Japan, either, and never did again.

The Japanese people in Vancouver were just the same as the people in Japan: they were a pain in the neck. Nowadays, we're scattered all over a big country, so you don't know who lives where, but then, we were all together in one place in Vancouver, so it was a really small world. When I got together with my present husband, I got criticized. I stood out, because I went here and there as a midwife. I even got attacked by the Japanese newspapers. And there's a newspaper right here in Toronto that was running me down. It just looked at things on the surface, and it said I was only living for myself. But it isn't as if I'd been seduced by another man and left my husband. I had no stain on my conscience, even though there were lots of men who would have led a girl astray. I'm not the type to be moved by that. But in those days the morality was: once you get married, by photos or any other way, then you have to put up with it till the end, whether you like it or not.

Right after coming to Canada, I started working as a midwife in the Japanese area of Vancouver. I was busy from that day on.

I had a good practice. Another midwife called Mrs T. was already working there, and if there was a place she couldn't go to, she would send me instead. I would go out in the morning and not come back till night, and spent the day going around Vancouver. There was work, so it took my mind off things. Being a midwife was just the right kind of work for me. If it hadn't been, I would have died for sure. I wouldn't be around now.

I met my present husband in Vancouver. He was about to leave for Japan to find a wife. I told him my troubles. He looked at me, and he understood right away. He saved me. His brother-in-law went to a lot of trouble for me too, and I was able to get remarried three years after I got to Canada. I got remarried about a year and a half after meeting this man. It was a marriage by free choice, but while we were seeing each other, our relations were clean.

My husband came to Canada in 1909 when he was 17, sent for by his brother-in-law. He's from Sakaiminato in Tottori Prefecture. His older sister and her husband had come to Canada early, and the brother-in-law was a sawmill contractor. He was a fine person; he could speak English and he had a big store too. Afterwards, though, he had trouble and went bankrupt. Then he took his whole family back to Japan. At the time, my husband made a lot of money for his sister and sent her back with it. When he was brought over, he was still very young, so he followed in his brother-in-law's footsteps and worked in the sawmill. At that time, "Japanese" and "sawmills" went together; there wasn't any other kind of work. When he married me, he was going around the countryside working in mills. They'd finished with one mountain, the sawmill would close, and they'd pack up and move on.

All the time I was in Vancouver I went on being a midwife. I was busy because that was the time the Nisei, the second generation, was being born, and I made a lot of money. I remember getting 50 dollars for delivering twins. After they had their babies, these women didn't have anybody to look after them, so

I'd go and see to them for about two weeks afterwards. I'd even wash diapers and do housework. In those days, 50 dollars was a lot of money. When it came to women from Okinawa, they needed interpreters when they were in labour, because you couldn't understand them.

Two or three Japanese midwives were working in Vancouver alone, but we didn't have fixed rates for a delivery. Suppose you spent two weeks going to and from, some people would give you 25 dollars, others 30, but 50 dollars was unusual. It all depended on their standard of living. They would give you the money in an envelope. I liked to save up a lot of them, then open them all at the same time. In some cases, where people were in real trouble, I did it for nothing. I mean, for women whose husbands had run away. There was no way people like that could give me anything. I was the one who would buy something and take it to them.

I worked for two years or more, and don't remember how many deliveries I made, but I was very busy. I put aside a lot of money, too. After I got married for the second time, that money got spent as we moved here and there. I spent it because I didn't feel like staying in Canada. About the time I stopped being a midwife to get married, a Japanese doctor brought a lawsuit, and it turned out that Japanese women had to go to the hospital to have babies. That was a little after 1920. If midwives could deliver babies, that meant less work for the doctors. That was why they campaigned and appealed to the government, and prevented midwives from practising if they didn't have Canadian midwives' qualifications. Afterwards, some midwives did keep working, but in secret.

It happened that my husband was going to a sawmill near Prince George, taking 30 Japanese with him, and that's when I quit working. I'd been about three years in Vancouver. I was sorry to stop being a midwife. There weren't many Japanese women in places like sawmills, and so it wasn't likely there'd be births. That's how I gave up making money, and started following my husband here and there.

Sawmill work lasted one or two years at the most, and about six months in the short term. We went to Swanson Bay, Shawnigan Lake, Prince George, and then my husband went to the Queen Charlotte Islands, too. He must have worked for 10 years or so until we settled down for good in Prince Rupert. Usually as a contractor, he would get some workers together, men from his own prefecture, and go to a place with a sawmill. My work was cooking and washing, and didn't amount to very much.

In Swanson Bay, our first son was born. There was a doctor in town, and I was a patient of his, but the labour pains came all of a sudden, and I had the baby before the doctor arrived. I knew all about it, so I got up and checked the umbilical cord, and cut it myself. My husband was no use at all, he just kept running in and out, saying, "It's a boy, it's a boy!" A neighbour came to help and give the baby his first bath.

In sawmill work, my husband did all kinds of things. He's the kind who can do anything. He came to Canada when he was young and worked at all kinds of things, he says. His family in Japan was in debt, so he used to send them money to help out, even just a little at a time. He worked 10 hours a day, and all year long without a holiday, to earn money. When he married me, he didn't have a cent because he was always sending money back to Japan.

At sawmills, it was the white men who worked as sawyers, the ones who decided what kind of boards to take from the logs, and gave the signal to start sawing, and they were the graders, the ones who looked at the quality of the lumber and classified it. The Japanese couldn't get work that needed skill. That's why their wages were much lower. If white people got two dollars a day, the Japanese got about $1.40: it was always 30 per cent lower. From hearsay, some white people would find out that my husband could work as a sawyer, and they would come to get him. When they offered him work, he'd ask for good wages above all else, and after that job he'd move on to another one. Wherever he went, he worked as a sawyer or a grader for high pay, and so he always made us a living. And he kept sending money back home.

Maybe the Japanese got low wages, but their cost of living was lower too. They could live on half of what white people needed. From Japan we could get cheap food, rice and fish, Japanese *hijiki* seaweed, dried tofu, kelp, and wakame seaweed. Expenses for food were low because we only ate meat about once a week. So as long as you were working, you didn't have any trouble. Though, we used to get told we had a "low standard of living" and that was one reason we got discriminated against.

No matter what company you worked for, they separated the workers by their race. The Japanese would only be with other Japanese, and most of them would be from the same area. The Chinese were with other Chinese. Among the whites, there were camps with Italians only, and they were looked on as a step below the other whites. Everybody was an immigrant, and no wonder they split up. The people with capital were the English Canadians, and they would use immigrants and pay them according to their race. In the Queen Charlottes, the Indians set up a sawmill, and said they wanted to hire Japanese sawyers, so my husband went to work there. He spent about two years there, using Indian workers only, but he didn't see any future in the job, so he quit. On the islands, there was one Japanese all alone, farming. He was brave, but he didn't manage to make a go of it.

What with going here and there, we had quite a few moving expenses. In fact, they came to a lot. We had no money left. My daughter was born, and I got tired of moving around with two children, and thought I'd like to settle down for about 10 years at least, even in a broken-down house. I was anxious, wondering what the future was going to be like, with us doing work like this. Even if we worked and worked and didn't do anything else, we wouldn't get anything out of it. I told my husband he should be a little more ambitious.

At last in 1924, we settled down as a family in Prince Rupert. Even at that, my husband just took Prince Rupert as a base, and went on doing migrant work. These days, Prince Rupert is the most important city in northern B.C., but when we went there, it was just a little town. Even so, about 50 Japanese families were already living there. There were shipwrights in town, and two restaurants, two barbers, three rooming houses, two groceries, and fishermen. In summer, the fishermen went to the Skeena River and the north to work, and in winter they came back to town. We lived here for nearly 20 years, till the war. The three children grew up here. It was a small town, so all the Japanese knew each other. Even now, the Japanese from Prince Rupert are close to each other, like relatives.

When my husband worked at the sawmill in Prince Rupert, he did the most important kind of work. It was milling all the lumber from one mountain. He was the foreman and did the contracting, and used lots of workers. We got a room in a big house with three stories, and I worked as cook and housekeeper. There were 30 to 60 workers, single men, going in and out all the time.

I got up at four in the morning to cook their three meals. The workers insisted on starting the day with rice. I'd start serving rice, miso soup and pickles. For lunch, I got some help to have the food ready at noon on the dot. We'd cook a dish with fish or meat. At three o'clock I'd start heating the bath. I was the last one to get into the bath every night, then I'd clean it. Between times I did the cleaning and washing, then I went to bed at one or two in the morning. My husband didn't help me at all; I did everything. It was my job to collect room and board money from the workers, too. Then I'd order the food; that was up to me too. I was able to do all of this because I was young, but looking back on it, it's a wonder I lasted even one or two years.

My husband was a contractor, so he really made good money. I used to get two dollars for meals and two for laundry from each worker. If I looked after 30 of them, that meant 120 dollars a month, it was good money. A lot of them were bachelors, they'd make jokes and they teased me: "It's nice just to have the young missus cooking for us."

But it wasn't easy to look after dozens of people and keep them under control. I knew very well how hard my husband was working. When we were eating together in the dining room, it was a trial to listen to complaining and grumbling every day. But my job was to listen to them. No matter what happened, I couldn't look angry. As you can imagine, the fishing grounds in the Skeena area were tough. They used to say, every year in the old days, there'd be Japanese killing each other.

And then, everybody would come trying to borrow money. "Can you lend me some, missus?" They knew I had some money, so I could hardly turn them down. After all, they returned it with interest when they won money gambling. If they lost, they wouldn't go to work. My husband would go and wake them up in the morning; that was a hard thing to do. There were lots of Chinese in town, and any number of gambling places. That's where they'd spend all their pocket money. I thought, this won't do, and I asked my husband to have them gamble at our place. The money changed hands over and over again, and for a while it was profitable, but that didn't last long.

By and by, the sawmill we worked for caught on fire and burned down. Somehow, that happened often at sawmills. My husband says there were a lot of arsonists around. The companies had insurance, tens of thousands of dollars, so when business went bad, they'd set fires to get the insurance money. The owners would do drastic things like that. We got burned out twice in Prince Rupert. The second time was just the same as the first. We were so disappointed. It was a sawmill, so the lumber really burned fast. We got burned out, with practically no clothes on. The second time, the insurance company came to check, and they went to court. In the end, the owner got charged with setting the fire, and he killed himself with a pistol. It was a big company he'd owned, with lots of workers; he was rich, an English Canadian. Rich people could be rough and dishonest. They'd do anything for business, just to raise the profits.

But in the end, we were the ones who got left holding the

bag. We didn't just get burned out, we had to take care of everything afterwards. My husband was the contractor, so he lent the workers some money and sent them back to Vancouver. That money didn't get returned, so we went broke. We lost all that money we'd been saving up. We didn't have any luck with money. It's true that some of them returned the money, but we couldn't push people to give it back, could we? In the old days we were generous. We didn't even ask for a piece of paper, we just lent out the money freely, and the money we earned all got spent by other people.

My husband dreamed of setting up his own sawmill, but he couldn't. It took a lot of capital. In those days, we had a little money to spare, and it was the time we could think of things like that. Our workers had families in Japan, so they'd send money back. As for their spending money, they gambled it away. I met lots of working people, but not one of them managed to save money. Those were good times for me, so I sent my mother 10 or 20 dollars at a time, asking her to pay visits to the shrine of the Konko religion. By the time my parents died, I'd sent them quite a lot of money.

Soon after we went broke from the fire, the Depression hit. That was a very rough time. A lot of people were on relief. The Japanese thought that going on relief meant getting help from somebody else, and they wouldn't ask for it until they needed it badly. If you applied at town hall you could get it, even if it was just a little. White people didn't mind asking for relief and they got lots of it. When parents were on relief, the children would say "relief, relief," like a chant. But the Japanese managed to live by helping each other out: the people they knew, the people they were close to.

We were out of money, so my husband finally found work as a fisherman, and I went out as a housekeeper. He bought a big boat, but he wasn't experienced, so he didn't catch very much. In those days he had a lot of trouble getting a licence, and after he did something for the Japanese Association, he finally got one.

The Japanese just did salmon fishing, but my husband couldn't rest easy if he only did the same work as other people. So he went away out into the Pacific to catch halibut. The Norwegian and Swedish fishermen used to do well at catching this fish, with their big boats, and my husband probably wanted to have a try.

When you get caught in a storm at sea, you risk your life. Since he was just going through the motions, copying the other fishermen, he nearly died, and that wasn't just once or twice. I didn't know anything about it. At last, he quit fishing. There were a lot of fish around Prince Rupert, but the government wouldn't let anybody take shrimp or crab. If you caught six-inch crabs, people wanted them, and they sold well. The government banned them, so there was a lot of illegal fishing.

Even during the Depression, we did all right without going on relief, but I wanted money, so I went out to work as a housekeeper. I worked five or six years in a sawmill manager's house. It was a beautiful house, all cypress. They had a washing machine: you didn't see many in those days, and I thought it was wonderful. In the bedrooms they had six Japanese folding screens, covered with gilt, but people like us couldn't ever have things like that. We lived in sawmill houses, or else we rented a house in town. I thought we could never own a place like this manager's house.

All the Japanese were renters. They lived in broken-down houses, but at least the rents were low. Our friend Mr Y. was a real pioneer, he'd come in a group to open up the area in 1907, when the town was first set up. It was completely wild land, and there wasn't a single house, they say. People lived in tents. Mr Y. had been a grocer at that time. As more and more people came to live there, his business grew, and he built a new store. All the Japanese who lived in Prince Rupert went to help him build a beautiful new house. As soon as it was built, the war came, and he had to leave it behind. No matter how hard you worked before the war, you couldn't live as the owner. That was the standard among the Japanese immigrants.

Our three oldest children grew up in Prince Rupert. When they got to be public school age, they'd pray morning and night. I grew up a Buddhist, but "when in Rome ..." as they say, and I thought they should pray. My son who died, he was a very strong Christian, and every day he'd read and study the Bible. So his parents had to read it, too. In Prince Rupert, the Anglican Church was doing missionary work among the Japanese.

My son became close to Reverend M., from Japan, and we got baptized, too, because of this man's influence. At first, there were only four or five baptized Japanese, but a white missionary came around to all our houses, giving Bible classes. You had to study and get to a certain point, then you were baptized. My oldest son was a good student, too, so he got chosen by Reverend M., and it was decided he'd be sent to Japan to become a minister.

Only five or six Japanese got baptized at the same time as me, and a lot of people laughed at us. Nowadays, all the Issei are Christians, but in those days they hated Christianity. Everybody said nasty things like, if you turned Christian, it was because you'd "sinned" a lot. People who said things like that all became Christians after the war. It's reached the point that it's embarrassing if you don't become a Christian. And the first time I went back to Japan, in 1953, I told my relatives I'd become a Christian. Until then it was a secret.

In my family in Japan, my younger brother held Buddhist services for the ancestors, but he'd read the holy book of the Konko religion too, and beat the drum of a Shinto god. He prayed for happiness for my husband and me, saying our names, though I told him he shouldn't. He said: "If you believe hard in a lot of religions, you'll get your reward from one of them or the other." That's what the Japanese are like. When my mother died, it seems she said she'd be happy to die suddenly, and that would be thanks to the Konko religion, so she asked my brother to believe in it. My brother followed her wishes and followed the Konko religion.

In Prince Rupert there was a Japanese organization called the *Kyowakai*, the "harmony association," and my husband was the permanent chairman. It set up a Japanese-language school and all the Japanese children went to it. The Anglican church had a kindergarten, and the Japanese children had to go to it. That was so they could learn English. The church was small, but it was the only Anglican Church, and that was a good thing, because if a little village had two or three churches, the Japanese couldn't get together. In the Anglican Church, the white missionaries tried to put the Japanese among the white people. They taught us all kinds of things, from the English language to etiquette, and they introduced us to white people's families. They did everything they could for the Japanese to assimilate to Canada. The Japanese owe those missionaries a big debt. I think that's why so few of the Prince Rupert Japanese had a pure Japanese style.

What the women had real trouble with was having so many children. Everybody had problems with all those children being born. There were some in trouble who came to see me. They knew I was a midwife, so they came to talk about family planning. They said it was funny that my husband and I didn't have many children. In the old days, even if you didn't want to have a child, you had to. When they came to have a talk with me, I couldn't be open, the way you can now, so I had trouble too, and I listened to them without saying anything. My husband is really somebody who likes to help other people, so he used to study my textbooks on midwifery and read books from Japan, and he made it a subject of conversation.

A little before World War II, when we had to leave Prince Rupert, we lost our oldest son. It was the summer just after he graduated from high school. He said he was going to earn money for university, and he went fishing as his father's partner. My husband almost never slept at night on board, but that night he dozed off, and our boy fell into the sea and drowned. He came up right away, but the water was so cold he couldn't be saved. In the north, even in summer, there's ice melting in the sea. That was the only time I was at the end of my rope, and I wished we'd died together. I asked my husband, "Why wasn't it you that died?" My son was 16 years old.

The high school principal said it was a great loss to the school, too. The minister from the white church, who'd been very kind to my son, cried along with me. My son's grave is in Prince Rupert. About 10 years ago, I visited his grave for the first time since the war. I remember what he said before he died, around the time the war was coming: the Japanese Canadians are Canadians, so it's natural for them to be loyal to this country. There I was, wanting to go back to Japan no matter what, so I was ashamed. Later on, I thought he was right.

The war began in 1941, and the next spring the government order came. We had to leave Prince Rupert inside a week. I don't recall much about those times, except for something the minister told the Japanese children: "It's so sad you have to leave because of the war. It's hard to separate," and he cried his eyes out. So did we. As for what happened afterwards, I've forgotten all about it, but I'll always remember what he said. I wished from the bottom of the heart there wouldn't be a war, because innocent children would have to be taken away. Then the news came from Japan that my younger sister's husband had died, and she'd been left a widow with two little children, and so I ended up hating the war.

But even when we were told to get out, I didn't get angry. I thought it was best we should be in a safe place, protected, because I was scared every day, people kept calling us "Jap." All the Prince Rupert Japanese took the train to Vancouver on the same day, then we got put in the camps. We got on the train without knowing where it would take us. I did think, "No matter where we're sent, surely the government won't let us starve." My youngest child, 11 years younger than the next one, was three years old, the only one that was on my hands. We were in the temporary camp at Hastings Park from March to August, waiting to get sent to a ghost town.

Right after we got to Vancouver, my husband started to agitate, saying he wanted to do some work that would help the government. He got the idea of mending shoes in a camp. There'd be hundreds of people, children included, so any number of shoes would get worn down. It happened that a man he'd done favours for in Prince Rupert was a shoemaker, and he was regarded as dangerous, so he got interned and put into a special camp for enemy aliens. My husband took over all the machinery and tools the man owned, and applied to the Commission for shoe repair work. They approved, and that's how my husband went to Tashme, where the biggest camp was, and became a shoemaker.

He got everything together in Vancouver, the machinery and the materials, before going to Tashme. He was lucky. He couldn't do shoe repairs, as he didn't know how, so he got some experienced men to do the work and made himself the boss. The rates for repairs were low, so everybody in the camp was happy; he was doing something for them. The Commission people trusted him, too, and they treated us well. So when we left Tashme, they told him he could take all the materials left over from the sewing machines, for free. He sent it all to Toronto as five tons of freight. At the time, he learned by observing, and got to learn shoe repair somehow or another, and thanks to that, when we resettled in Toronto, he carried on as a shoemaker for six years.

In Tashme, my husband worked as a shoemaker, I was a midwife, and our daughter taught school. We all got the same pay, 25 cents an hour, about 45 dollars a month. Even in the camp, people had babies. Maybe 400 or 500 Nisei were born there. There were about 4,000 Japanese in Tashme, so we had everything: schools, a hospital, bathhouses and a shoe repair place. The two of us midwives took turns working day or night shifts, and we were very busy. My husband was the boss of the shoe repair shop, and he didn't do anything, just counter work, so he could take it easy. He organized a baseball team and for three whole years he was the manager. He worked all right, but he liked to have fun, too.

If you worked an hour, it was a flat 25 cents, and I put in all the time I could, so I got good pay. In camp, most people hung around doing nothing. Their excuse was that they were prisoners, but a midwife can't be idle. I worked like mad, and I think it was all to the good. Because of my work, I didn't get bored. We were isolated, but it wasn't like being in Japan; we didn't fear for our lives. Only, getting along with the other Japanese was a trial. A year or two after coming to the camp, everybody got wrought up, and the so-called "judo groups" lorded it over everybody, and they were frightening.

My husband knew what was right and wrong, and he stuck to his guns. People who thought like him would come to our place. Then, there were always some contrary people who wanted their own way. Sometimes, before a meeting at our place, he'd post a watchman on the corner. I hated this, Japanese against Japanese, even more than not being able to go outside the camp. We insisted that our children were getting protected, so we'd better do what the Commission wanted. Then, we got criticized for being traitors. But if you look at people who said that sort of thing, their children got to grow up in the camp, and now they're fine people. We were thinking of our children before anything else, so it was just a "yield to the powerful" situation; that's all we could do.

It would have been bad for the children to do nothing for four years or more and end up as idlers, so we set up a parents' association and asked the government for all kinds of things. My husband was very active in this group. Some Nisei soldiers from Toronto, they'd joined the Canadian army, came to visit the camp, but the *gambariya*, the resistors, wouldn't have anything to do with them. I gave the soldiers a place to stay. And some people didn't like that, either.

My husband urged the young people to go east as soon as they could. When it came time to sign up for "repatriation," he went around advising people to stay in Canada. And again, that brought on a lot more criticism. There were all kinds of fights and squabbles; he helped out people who got involved in lawsuits, too. In a place like that, people's real feelings come out. You meet all kinds of mean people, cruel people showing their true faces, and I've never understood people's feelings as well as I did in those days. In the end, the right side won out, and from the third year things settled down. The women were lucky, they did good things like sewing, cooking, and flower arranging.

Then it came time to sign up for "repatriation." My husband was very active talking against it. He walked around lecturing people, trying to talk them out of it. For a moment, a lot of people got taken in by smooth talk from government people, and came around to the idea of going to Japan. The government said it would pay 200 dollars in expenses per person in a family, and if you had five children, it would have come to $1000. The people who signed up got lured by this money. Once people got the idea of going, they certainly didn't feel like staying on here. My husband went around trying to prevent people from leaving. At times he even sent for a minister and had him try to persuade these people. All this was going on, then the war ended.

It was 1946 when we came to Toronto. We brought the two youngest children. We'd closed the shoe repair shop in Tashme and had all our things sent here. For a while we lived in a small rented place. My husband walked around every day looking for a house, but nobody wanted to sell or rent to a Japanese. No matter how much money you had, they wouldn't sell. After a year and a half, just by chance, something came in handy, a letter of recommendation from the Anglican minister in Tashme that my husband had kept around, and we happened to get this house. It was a real stroke of luck. My husband opened a shoe repair shop here. I wanted to open some kind of business too, and found a place a block down from here, and started a coffee shop with my daughter. Those were the days when coffee was ten cents a cup. A lot of students would come in, and we made over a hundred dollars a day. When my daughter got married I couldn't manage alone, so I sold the shop within two years.

I was in my prime, I'd just turned 50, and wanted to do something more important, to succeed. That was my dream when I left Japan. The coffee shop wasn't bad, but I wanted to do something a little different, and I advised my husband to open a Japanese restaurant. When I told my husband to get ambitious again and do something big, his spirits picked up.

We spent the money we had on hand and borrowed some more to put the capital together. That was 30 years ago, when white people didn't know anything about Japanese food. I'd heard of five or six restaurants in New York, so we went there and studied the menus. We found that *sukiyaki* and *tempura* appealed to white people. I was so glad when we opened. That's why I worked so hard. My husband did the managing, and I looked after the kitchen. Some of our workers quit, saying they couldn't keep up with me. "If we work like her, we'll die." Sometimes I'd go in at nine in the morning and come home at one, two, even four the next morning. I was skin and bones. I worked and worked, as hard as I could.

Our first year we went into the red. When we paid the chef, we used to give him all the cash on hand out of the proceeds. After two or three years, the customers started coming in, and I was so relieved. I'd been thinking what trouble I'd be in, if we went bankrupt. I kept thinking I didn't want to give in, or get laughed at.

Fortunately, our sons are doing well in the business now, but they've got competition, so it's no holiday. We were pioneers, but Japanese food has been talked about, so it's popular with white people now. So that was nice.

When I was young, I wanted to do everything by myself. I wanted to succeed. So I had lots of incentive. I never forgot that I'd come all the way to Canada, and I couldn't stand still. I think I've done pretty well for myself. Nowadays I don't want for anything, but I don't have the energy I used to have, so it's a bit sad.

My husband is never at home. Ever since he was young, he's loved to go out, and he says he can't go to bed until he's seen street lights outside. He doesn't do anything around the house. He looks fine on the outside, but at home he doesn't say anything.

He can't drink, but he likes entertainment; he just loves the horse races, and even now he goes to the track a lot. He's lucky, he's done everything he wanted to. He got cancer 20 years ago, but they found out early and he was completely cured. Even when he gets sick, he's lucky!

We used to visit Japan a lot, but we can't now, we're 90 years old. All the people we knew are dead, and I get sadder and sadder. My husband likes to do things for people, and that's going to last till the end. He took care of all the funeral arrangements for the Prince Rupert people who died here in Toronto. As for our funerals, he says the Nisei born in Prince Rupert will look after them. We're the very last people from the old days.

I suffered because of my frizzy hair, and thought that if I went overseas I wouldn't have to wear a pompadour.

Mrs Tami Nakamura

5 Mrs Tami Nakamura

Mrs Tami Nakamura is spending her retirement with her husband who will be 93 years old this year, in a country town about 250 miles from Toronto. The area around the town, on the shore of Lake Erie, is a thriving place for greenhouse vegetables and potted flowers, and there is a good-sized city nearby. Since this region is at the southernmost tip of Canada, the climate is relatively mild, and in summer, cool winds blow across the lake. As a place for retirement, Mrs Nakamura says, a country locale like this one is ideal for her husband, who, with his love of farming, has cultivated land all his life.

Their second son, who has carried on his father's occupation, and their third son, who works for a company, live nearby with their own families. Thus, they can be called on in case of emergency. At present, however, Mrs Nakamura is looking after her own household. Her work consists of: caring for her husband who has recently become seriously infirm; gathering vegetables from the household garden which is really a good-sized field; and preparing three meals a day. She seems to be thinking that she is fulfilling her last duties. She is at the advanced age of 85, and on top of that, she is physically slight, weighing just under eighty pounds (36 kilos). Even so, she has no disabilities, so that every time the family doctor examines her, he looks at her in amazement. Mrs Nakamura says she has never taken any medicine.

Her husband, who crossed the Pacific Ocean with a dream of operating a big farm, can be called the classic type of the Issei who came to Canada around the beginning of this century. These days, no matter how hard one looks throughout the country, it is extremely difficult to find any survivors among the pioneers who lived through the land-clearing period. At the early age of 17, this youth, attracted by the idea of vast lands in Canada, decided to become a large-scale farmer. Had it not been for World War II and the uprooting of the Japanese Canadians from the west coast, Mr Nakamura might have fulfilled his dream. Today, the fruit and vegetables from the farmland cleared by Issei farmers like Mr Nakamura would be producing in abundance, filling the markets of the whole country.

As a city girl, brought up in Hiroshima, the picture-bride-to-be expected to marry a big farmer, and never planned to crouch over the fields herself, picking strawberries and digging potatoes. Even so, after more than 60 years of marriage, both husband and wife say that they have no regrets at all for a life spent on the land, even to the smallest detail.

The Nakamuras are probably typical of Japanese Canadian families who lived the postwar period in the spirit of "let's move forward; let's be positive." When they resettled in Eastern Canada, the family made a conscious decision to live apart from other Japanese Canadians, and to start over again from a position within Canadian society at large. Mrs Nakamura firmly believes that they did well to adapt to their new territory, putting the past behind them, with the thought that it was all the fault of the war, and that, at the very least, this was a big advantage for the future of their children and grandchildren. We can say that many of the Japanese Canadians who resigned themselves and rapidly made a fresh start wherever they resettled belonged to the Success Group, and are living out their lives in a spirit of calm. For the Unforgetting Group who were not able to shed their resentment at being treated as enemy aliens, the postwar years held nothing for them but dissatisfaction and bitterness.

For the Nakamuras, it was surely a severe trial to start all over again when they had been stripped of everything. In fact, their path must have been full of stumbling-blocks. Here is a point to consider: the land that the Nakamuras abandoned so easily "with no regrets at all," the 40 acres in Mission in the Fraser Valley, with its fine climate and scenery, is now prime farmland, and its monetary value is unquestioned. To give up "with no regrets" is perhaps a peculiarly Japanese skill. Or perhaps, because they had had such a painful life before the war as poor "second-class citizens" that they wanted to forget it as soon and as completely as possible, they renounced everything they possessed without regrets.

There was something else the Japanese Canadians could never regain, besides the land and possessions they left behind in British Columbia. Something else, perhaps more precious, disappeared forever: the sense of a shared fate, the sense that "we all used to help each other out, we were together in sad times and happy times." Mrs Nakamura traces her memories of the relationships among the approximately 40 Japanese families in Mission in tones of indescribable warmth. As she spoke, the true spirit of community within this small group, with their understanding of each other deepened by common experience, brought out feelings of nostalgia not in Mrs Nakamura, but in me, as I talked with her.

Both the Nakamuras are from Hiroshima Prefecture originally, but Mrs Nakamura speaks standard Japanese to people from other parts of Japan. Her calm and methodical nature is perfectly reflected in the accuracy of her words and in her command of formal speech.

My family is from Hiroshima, but since my father was a military man, I was born in Kumamoto, where he was posted.

It was in 1896, the 29th year of Meiji. Then we went to Kagoshima, and about four years later we moved back to Hiroshima, it seems. My father was an officer, a lieutenant, but he didn't carry a rifle; after he went to paymasters' school, he worked in the Accounting Section at Headquarters. In Hiroshima, we lived at the Fifth Divisional Headquarters near the Castle, and I grew up there.

In Hiroshima there was an officers' club called the Kaikosha, and it operated a school for the children of officers, right on the parade ground. It was tuition-free for children of officers below the rank of captain, and as my father was a lieutenant, I got my schooling for free when I entered the Kaikosha's Seibi School. I went there till graduation six years later. When I took the exam for the prefectural school for girls, I placed near the bottom of the class, but I got in anyway, and went to the girls' high school for four years. At school, you could take either English or Embroidery as an optional subject. At the time I never dreamed of coming over here, so I chose Embroidery, and didn't study English in Japan. After high school, I stayed at home.

In those days, nobody worked even if they'd graduated from girls' school. A woman just got married. If you said you were going to be a working woman, you got laughed at. In the Hiroshima area, some women became schoolteachers, nurses, or telephone operators. But that was just until they got married. I used to see young women walking past our house morning and night, going to work. They were all wearing *hakama* (Japanese-style divided skirts). If women had been free to work, like today, I would have tried it too, without getting married. But I just went to girls' school where all they gave you was a bride's education. So when I graduated I was like everybody else; I took lessons in sewing and the *koto* (a Japanese harp). If I started wanting to go overseas, it was because of a silly reason.

I've never told anybody about this before, but ... It's because I wasn't good-looking. That isn't very flattering to my husband, but there it is. Besides my face, there's my frizzy hair, as you see, and it's dreadful. It's thin now, so it isn't noticeable, but it's terribly kinky. When I was a young girl in Japan, the fashion was smooth upswept hair; they had different pompadour styles, and my hair wasn't right for any of them. I suffered so much, I got to feel that I couldn't get married, and that's why I started wanting to go overseas.

One of my classmates had gone to Hawaii, and said to come, because she'd look after me. At the time I didn't like the idea of Hawaii very much. I must have had a vague dream of going to a place like the United States or Canada. So I wasn't unwilling to emigrate, in fact I really wanted to come here. I didn't care what my husband would be like. I didn't even have marriage in mind. As long as I could go, that was all I wanted. I just wanted to go to a foreign country, because I wouldn't have to wear a pompadour. Nowadays, you're lucky to have frizzy hair even in Japan; you don't need a permanent, but in those days it just wouldn't do. That was my reason for wanting to leave Japan.

At the time, you couldn't come over unless you were married. No matter how much you wanted to, it was impossible to come alone. Any husband would do, so all I had to do was get married. Two or three years after I graduated, my father became ill and died, and my mother had to make do with an officer's pension, and take care of the household. If I got married, that would take some of the burden off my mother. Besides, I could work overseas and send money back to her. I was the oldest of five children, my brothers and sisters were at home, and I came to realize how hard life was, so I felt I wanted to help out, if only a little. If my father had been alive, I think he would have been against the idea.

Just then an acquaintance of my mother's came along, saying that a certain man she knew wanted a wife. He was a farmer in Canada, and according to his father, he was doing well, so I wouldn't have to do anything but housework. So I thought, well, maybe I'll get married, and agreed. The arrangements went ahead. My father-in-law was pleased with me and took the trouble of coming to our house, and said he wanted this marriage to happen. So the discussions went ahead and I got engaged. I didn't meet the man; I just saw his photos.

Then we exchanged letters for six months. My husband often wrote, but there's nothing special that I remember. I don't remember anything of what I wrote, either. I do remember that his letters gave me the impression that he wasn't a bad person. Anyway, it was my feeling that I could get married to anybody, so I wasn't particular about details. I thought that if I were to live in a town in Canada, I could work too and send at least a little money to my mother. When I arrived, I found he was very, very poor and there was no question of sending her any.

My husband grew up in Hiroshima City, actually a place on the coast called Eba-cho about a mile from the centre of the city. It was a place where they harvested laver and oysters, and his family did a little fishing along with the farming, and they had a nice house. They were on the prosperous side, I think. My father-in-law was working, without expecting any money from overseas. It seems my husband had thought of going abroad from the time he was a child, and he left the village with a friend when he was 17. A lot of immigrants went from the Eba area to Hawaii, intending to make a success of themselves. They say quite a few went to the U.S. mainland, too.

So it seems he went to Hawaii first, worked for about six months on a sugar-cane plantation, and then came to Canada in 1907. He worked in road construction, and sawmills, and learned English by working in a hotel. At the time he came over his dream was to own a farm, so he saved everything he earned, he says. With the little money he saved by practically starving, he went west, from the area of Vernon in the interior of British Columbia, walking around looking for farmland. That was the third year after he came to Canada. He got 20 acres of uncleared land in Mission. He cleared it, and finally by the time he sent for me he was growing a few strawberries on it.

The marriage talks had gone ahead, and our parents had approved, so I had entered my husband's family register and was living at their house. When I got registered, all we did was to decorate the place with my husband's photo, invite relatives and neighbours, and hold a sort of mock marriage ceremony. I didn't bring anything with me, and lived with my in-laws without doing anything. Six months after I had married into the Nakamura family, my passport was issued. I left Japan in October 1916.

I was 21 and when time came to set out, I got happier and happier because at last I was going off to a place I'd been dreaming of for so long. There was no reason to learn about what kind of man I had married. I wasn't afraid, thinking that once I got there it would be all right. The only slight worry I had was, he was a farmer, while I had grown up in the city. I was right to worry. I came to a farm, and had a hard time of it. As a housewife I worked from sunup to sunset, cooking, washing, and bringing up the children; eventually more than 10 people were living in that farmhouse all the time, including people we brought over from Japan, and the hired men, so my work never ended.

I left Japan from Kobe, and my mother-in-law saw me off. I was already the bride, so my father-in-law paid for everything: the passage and expenses. I even got spending money. He was very nice and encouraged me all he could. I made friends with two other brides going to Canada from Kobe, just like me, and the three of us had a lot of fun; it was just like a school outing. One of them had married a man who was farming on Vancouver Island, but she had built him up too much in her imagination, and after she got to Victoria, she cried, saying she didn't know her husband was such an old man. There was no going back, but she didn't want to get off the ship either, so it was a problem. That was the peak of picture marriages, so the boat was full of brides, and we made a lot of commotion. It was a small ship called the *Sadomaru*, and it took two weeks to get to Victoria.

My husband had come to meet me from Mission in the country and later I was told that he had gone to a movie in Vancouver. It was so interesting that he wanted to see it again, and when he did, he missed the ferry to Victoria, so he came alone after the others. I didn't mind that he wasn't there, because all the brides were looking at the men, saying "whose husband is that?" Anyway, the whole ship was full of brides and they were terribly excited.

When I saw him for the first time, I thought his face was quite a bit nicer than in the photos. He was smiling a big smile. Well, it was our first meeting, so he must have been happy. As for me, I wasn't especially glad. I didn't think the marriage was good or bad. I thought "Well, this is the man I've married." For his personality, just as I had thought, he was a nice man and I had nothing to complain about. We stayed at a hotel for one night, and the next day we took the ferry to Vancouver. I got new Western clothes made from head to toe and wore them all the way to Mission.

Mission is on the north shore of the Fraser River, 40 miles from Vancouver. We took the train there and at the station a horse and wagon came for us. I'd been imagining that my husband was a big farmer with 20 acres of land in Mission, but as I was taken along into the mountains I wondered what kind of place Mission was, and where we were going. There were certainly some big fields, and houses too, but it was much wilder than I had imagined it in Hiroshima. It was real frontier country.

My husband had three live-in farmhands. Since we were coming, they had cooked a special meal and were waiting for us. I remember that one of the boys who wore a headband was from Wakayama. He bowed, and welcomed me in his dialect. It was the custom among the Japanese in Mission that every time a new bride came, all the neighbours would show up suddenly to tease the couple. It was to say "Congratulations," I suppose. We didn't know, but when we went to bed, around nine o'clock everybody came around making a terrific noise. So we got up and dressed and hurried around serving them drinks. They stayed a short while and then went home. There were about 20 Japanese households in Mission, and we were a cosy group; we got along well and helped each other out. We never had a bit of trouble.

The land my husband owned was a good 20 acres, but it was on a wild mountain. When he bought it, the price was $50 per acre, so it cost him a thousand dollars. He paid one-quarter of that in cash, and was paying off the rest with a small amount every year. None of the land was flat; it was all mountain, and the Japanese would go up the mountainside gradually, clear it and make it into farmland. If you went further inland, there were sawmills making ties for the railway. The 20 acres my husband bought later with Mr U. was the same kind of wild mountain land, and they cleared it, but it took some very heavy labour.

First they would cut down everything in the bush; trees were growing all over. Then they would dig out the roots, pile them up, and burn them, to make it clear. Since they used dynamite, some men got killed when they didn't run away in time. When I got there, some people were still living in temporary shacks, but a good number of others had built houses and there were about 20 Japanese households working approximately five acres each.

Since I was coming, everything in the house needed for the time being was ready. The second floor was for the young people to sleep in, and downstairs there was a living room and kitchen, and our room. In the back, where the eaves went out, we made a big dining room. The lighting was with lamps, there was nothing electrical at all. We were in the mountains, so at least we could get lots of firewood. We had a big wood stove, and on top of it I did things like making toast, and boiling water for the wash. We owned two horses for clearing the land, and about 20 chickens that we got eggs from. There was a half-ton truck; later on, we bought a one-ton truck. I thought, well, this is what a farmer's house is like, and wasn't surprised.

Even in the towns around Vancouver, you didn't find any Japanese living in nice houses. I even had friends living on the second floor of a stable. Our farm had a Japanese bath outside. To fill it, we'd carry water in buckets from a well, and heat it. Everybody else would take a bath, and I'd be the last to get in. The next day, I'd pour in some fresh water. Nowadays I wouldn't bother for a moment with chores like that, but when you're young, you adapt. I was glad to do everything.

My husband has a good character; he's gentle. He does everything he can for the children, and for his workers, too. He doesn't drink or smoke, and he's sincere. So there weren't any lies in those letters he wrote me while we were engaged. I've got to call myself lucky. He has no hobbies; he's never cared about anything but working in the fields, and he was there from morning to night. He wanted me working there too; he was always saying "Come out, come out." Besides that, he was very understanding, and soon after I arrived, he let me go out to work as a housekeeper.

I went to Mission in October and at the beginning of December, I went to Vancouver to work as a housekeeper. I said I wanted to do that during the winter-time when there was no farm work, because I wanted to see how white people lived, and what their households were like. Anyway, in the mountains, even if you wanted to learn English, all you heard was Japanese, so you had no chance at all. My husband agreed with my idea, and took me to Vancouver. An agent found me work in a big house owned by rich people named Cummings, a house on Broadway. It was a beautiful house, and I got to study housekeeping.

They had guests at Christmas and New Year's, so they hired a special cook, and we made dinners together. It was nice because I learned a lot, but in February, my husband started getting busy, and he came to fetch me. I'd been there only three months, but I got $15 dollars a month. It didn't do anything for my English, but it was a good thing to do, I think. So I went home to Mission after three months, and in March I think it was, I was pregnant with my first son. I remember that in May, in the strawberry season, I had terrible morning sickness.

In four months, May to September, all kinds of strawberries come out, one after the other. Those months, it's war. My work was cooking and supervising meals for the pickers. I'd get up at four in the morning, cook rice and miso soup, and feed everybody. It was food for 40 people at least, so we had a cook, but it was a lot of work just to manage the house. Anyway, I was busy, busy every day and I had no spare time at all.

The year I came was in the middle of World War I, so times were good for farmers. If you grew strawberries and raspberries, they sold well. In the four years of the war, a lot of money must have come in. There were even some Japanese farmers on Vancouver Island who got rich quick on strawberries, they said. My husband had just started, but he was doing quite well for himself. We had three live-in farmhands, but when the season came he would hire a lot of extra help, and the times were so good it made him want to do even more. I was the one who had a rough time, though. I wonder how I held out, being pregnant so often.

Every year it was the same work, and come to think of it, we did it for 25 years, so we must have done pretty well. Even now, when Mission people get together, they always talk about those days. The women say that just thinking about it gives them the shivers. It was the same hard life for all the housewives. In winter there was some free time, relatively speaking, but even so, we always had people staying at our house. So I had to take care of them. I used to think I'd like to live with just my children.

There was always somebody staying with us, who went to work in the mountains. Some people came to pick strawberries in summer and stayed on afterwards. Some of them were stowaways, too. They'd stow away on the boats, then hide in the mountains to work, giving us false names. I wouldn't know until an immigration officer came to check up. In the end, some would be caught and they'd be taken away. Anyway, all kinds of people were forever going in and out, and I used to make their three meals a day, and do their washing. There were no machines in those days, so I scrubbed away with my hands.

For meals we had Japanese food, rice and miso soup. Sometimes for lunch I would broil salmon that the local Indians used to come selling in secret, and for the rest, I would cook vegetables from the fields. Once a week we could buy food, such as dried lotus root and burdock root, *hijiki* seaweed, tofu, and *kamaboko* (boiled fish paste) from a peddler from Vancouver. As long as you had money you could buy anything. My job was cooking more than anything else; day after day I would cook rice from morning on, all year long without stopping.

We worked like mad, but so much money went out in wages that we saved nothing at all. Even at the end of the year, we couldn't pay all the bills. It was always borrowing, borrowing money, and whenever the manager of a store in Vancouver came collecting, it was difficult. At the time there weren't any cars, so he would come by train, and whenever we spotted them marching up to the house, we'd panic. We'd always give him just a little money for part of the bill and send him away. For rice and soy sauce we'd pay once a year, and that was a lot of money. It would come to about $5,000, big money in those days, so we simply couldn't pay all at once.

At the end of the first season, and as the second year was coming around, I understood that we were poor, so I gave up the idea of making money and going back to Japan. I wanted to see my mother and brothers and sisters, but every year, I felt more and more resigned, and I got used to feeling like that. I had baby after baby, and Japan seemed further and further away. A farmer has land, so you get tied down to it and you settle in.

During the time we were in Mission, we had seven children. Luckily, Mrs H next door had been a midwife in Japan, so she always came and delivered them. All the Japanese children born in Mission were delivered by Mrs H. I'm really thin now, but I must have had a strong constitution. I was healthy; at school, I used to run fast in races, and I played tennis. So I never had one difficult delivery. The work was so hard and I was so busy that my milk gave out and I went over to bottle-feeding. Our children grew up healthy, but they have a small build. Maybe it's because they were on cow's milk. When the babies got a little bigger, I used to put them in a small box and take them out into the fields, and they were beside me as I picked berries. We lived on a farm, so we never wanted for food, but we were really poor. I wonder what our annual income was. I don't care very much about things like that. It was my husband's work to support us, but his pockets were always empty. From year to year, the price of strawberries would go up or down, depending on the yield, and that gave us a lot of trouble. When there was a long spell of good weather the crop would be ready too soon, and that put a stop to high prices after just a little while. In some years, like during the war, high prices went on for a long time, but when the war ended, nothing sold any more. When times were hard, the prices went down to practically nothing, and we really had problems. So instead of berries, we used to plant things like hops for beer and apple and plum trees. My husband liked to do all kinds of things.

All year round, over the years, we would have seven, eight, at the most ten people staying with us. We'd give them three meals a day and $15 a month; it amounted to giving them spending money. All year long there was some kind of work in the fields, and some of these men would always be hanging around. The only fun they got was gambling, and on Sundays they'd always go to the Chinese gambling place in Mission. If you didn't let them go, you had no peace of mind. On those days everybody got driven to town in a truck, and they'd be picked up again when they were finished.

For relaxation, all they did was gamble. Usually, at night they used to play cards. It was strange about the Chinese gambling places; they existed in every town. The police must have known about it, but it seems if they got a little money they'd look the other way. Once in a while somebody would hurry up in a taxi: "Boss, I lost everything. Can you lend me about five dollars?" and go off again with the money. That was no good, losing all their small wages, fifteen dollars. All of these men had come to

Canada to work and make money, but none of them had enough to send back to Japan. There weren't any that bought land and became independent. Even after 10 years, they were still migrant workers, and they ended up that way. So a lot of them went back during the war.

The people we brought over were different. The immigration rules got more and more strict, and it got to the point that the only people let in were farmers who were sent for from Canada. My husband got one to come every year. He brought over more than 10 people in all, his younger brother and cousins, my younger brother, and also some young men he knew. They used to work at our place for a year, and then leave. The men used to get $15 dollars a month, too, and afterwards all of them sent for wives. Some of them came through as farmers, and the others, the ones who weren't farmers, they scattered here and there. My brother, for example, wasn't suited to farming, so he went to Vancouver and opened a food store. All of them aimed at being independent, and somehow they managed. I don't think any of them went back to Japan because of the war.

That's why we always had a big household, with our family, the people we sent for, and the live-in farmhands. After berry-picking was over, we'd all go to Vancouver to have some fun. Just at this time of year, the Pacific National Exhibition would be on, so we'd all pile into the truck and go off. The children looked forward to the PNE so much that they'd save their pocket money all summer long. We used to stay in town two or three days and then come back. When we got home, it was no fun at all for the rest of the year. Then the men would start gambling again.

A lot of workers would come just for the berry season from May to September. These people got low wages. I'd guess that we paid about five cents per pound of strawberries they picked. We built big bunkhouses for these workers. There were Indians, Chinese, whites and Japanese all working together.

The Indians came from their villages with their children in groups of 10 or 20, so my husband would go to pick them up in his truck. They lived in a bunkhouse for Indians only. The Chinese lived apart with other Chinese, and cooked for themselves, and when berry-picking was over, they'd go home. Every year, like clockwork, when the season came, they would come around. White people would come in groups of four or five, they were unemployed. The races lived apart from each other for the season and acted differently, but we never had a bit of trouble. My husband could never bring himself to turn away people who said they wanted to work, and everyone was welcome. We had high school students coming from Vancouver, too, looking for jobs. Anyway, all kinds of people came, and after a season of work, they'd go home.

After we'd paid the workers and subtracted expenses, there wasn't much left. When there was some, it was quite a bit better, so we were able to borrow money here and there. We often borrowed in advance from the Farmers' Association. When the strawberries were ready we would pay off the debt, but sometimes we had to put it off to the next year. For our oldest son's expenses at university, we borrowed from the association, too. Maybe some people managed without borrowing, but from the time I went to live in Mission, I never heard of anyone who made money on strawberries: there were more people who borrowed. I should have done some bookkeeping and written down what happened, but at any rate we were busy, and I'll bet not even my husband remembers how much our income or expenses came to.

Around Vancouver, it seems there was a lot of discrimination. Japanese fishermen caught too many fish, so they got excluded. But among farmers, I never heard of anything like that. I never felt prejudice against Japanese. Some non-Japanese came to work at our place, but we never even heard of one fight, that's how well the races got along. The neighbours were white people, and farmers; they were very nice. If our English had been a little better, or if we'd been able to drink liquor, we would probably have visited back and forth, but in the 25 years we were in Mission we never had any white friends to meet with.

One reason there wasn't any discrimination in Mission was that whites and Japanese were in the same strawberry producers' association. Strawberries were all shipped out from the association at the same price. In the produce season, they were sent east of Mission as far as Calgary, and everything went through the association. When strawberries were sold to jam producers, the association negotiated prices and sold them collectively. So the races weren't likely to go up against each other on account of their interests.

I never heard of people not selling land to a Japanese, either. Only, it's sure there was a big difference in the yield of strawberries according to the way you farmed, even if you were growing them on one acre. The Japanese were better at growing strawberries. They say that white people couldn't grow but half as much as the Japanese could on one acre. That could make them jealous, and it might have caused some competition, but not in Mission. When the Japanese were driven out by the war, though, it seems berry-raising went way downhill.

There were more and more Japanese in Mission, and by wartime, 40 families. Everybody got along with each other, and we did a lot of visiting. We lived in the same village for nearly 30 years, so we helped each other out; it was like a family, and it was good like that. The centre of it all was the Japanese Farmers' Association. Everybody belonged to it. They used to get together and discuss farming. My husband worked hard at setting up this group, and he was the head for two terms, or 10 years. Everybody cooperated, so there was no trouble at all. As for religion, a lot of people were Buddhists, and they had their own church from very early on. Weddings, funerals and socials were at the Buddhist hall.

Our group of Christians got started a long time after that, but even then, the Japanese groups didn't wall themselves off from each other. We were friendly until the war separated us. The Farmers' Association bought land and built a hall on it. This hall was the centre for Japanese activities: there was a Japanese language school and a judo club for young people. When the children were old enough to go to school, they had a problem because they didn't know English. When my oldest son started primary school, he didn't speak any English and couldn't follow classes. That was only natural, because in Japanese families we didn't speak a word of English.

In a panic, we sent our son to a white family, and had him go to school from their house. Then the Association set up a kindergarten, hired a white teacher, and had her teach English. The farmhands from Japan that we had sent for, they went to night school, too, and learned English. So the Nisei learned English starting from kindergarten, and when they started primary school they went to Japanese classes after hours. It was quite an ordeal for them. Our place was a few miles away from the Japanese school, but our children all went to it.

Christianity must have come to the Mission Japanese in the 1920s. It started when a Japanese minister from Vancouver came once a month, and preached to four or five people. He held house meetings, and we were invited too, but my husband didn't know anything about Christianity, so he said "You go," and so I went for a while by myself. One time when Reverend A came from Vancouver, my husband went along too. Then, I don't know what happened, but my husband was so impressed by the minister that he started saying he wanted to be baptized right away: that was a surprise to me.

Since my husband's family was Buddhist, I thought it was best not to get baptized while his parents were living. But my husband is stubborn, and once he says he'll do something, there's no stopping him. He became a firm believer from that chance meeting with Reverend A, and with the three oldest children, we went to the Japanese church in New Westminster, and got baptized. From that time my husband became very serious about it, and stuck to his beliefs.

Reverend A was a fine person, who made a lot of believers among the Japanese, and not just in Mission. At first, we were a small group, and borrowed a white people's church. Gradually we all became very serious and little by little more people joined us, and we collected contributions to build a church. It was a beautiful church, but we used it only two or three times, because the war broke out. The Women's Association had started too, and met in the church only once, before we scattered. We all cried when we separated.

In the 1930s when our children grew up, it was the Depression, and the price of strawberries went down, and also we lowered the farmhands' wages. Our land had grown to 40 acres, and we were busy growing apples and potatoes. It was "no rest for the poor," as the saying goes, and somehow we managed to live on borrowed money. My husband said that no matter how hard it was for us, he would take care of the children's education, so they kept on going to school. Well, maybe we were better off than a lot of others. The children, once they were old enough, went into the fields and worked hard.

When we sent our son to the University of Washington, we put together his school expenses by getting an advance from the Farmers' Association. Our boy was certainly the first among the Japanese to go as far as university, before the war. It was 1935, the middle of the Depression, and everybody was amazed when we said he was going all the way to Seattle. The University of Washington students used to make a lot of money in summer, fishing in Alaska. But our boy came home the day the summer holiday began, and helped out. Even now, he seems to appreciate the chance he got. He writes letters saying that if everything went well, it was thanks to his father.

Luckily, we didn't have to send money back to Japan. There were a lot of people in Mission who did. Some sent money back, planning to return themselves. At my in-laws' house, nobody had money problems, so there was no need to help them out, and we never sent them any. As for my family, since my mother was getting along alone, I wanted to send her a little, but I couldn't. Instead, I sent for my younger brother and sister. My brother had never farmed, but we sent for him as a farmhand, and he stayed a year with us. We sent my sister travel expenses so she could come as a domestic worker, and she worked in Mission for about two years. She got married to a man living in Kelowna, and left Mission. I felt sorry about my mother, as the three of us were living in Canada. Even if we were poor, the living over here was better because you felt so relaxed, and it was better to educate the children here, too. I myself never thought of going back to Japan.

Eventually the war came, and it was horrid. My husband had become a citizen a long time before that, so we worried that he would be drafted into the Canadian army. We were nervous, but found out that farmers wouldn't be drafted, so we were relieved for a short while. We felt that if he were called up, he would have to go, because he had become a Canadian. It wasn't so much that he was devoted to Canada from the bottom of his heart, it was rather that he thought a citizen had a duty to serve. Since my husband had lived here for 30 years, and since he had become obligated here, it seemed natural for him to give service to Canada. His reasoning went that far, but feelings were something else again.

Afterward, during the war, our second son, who was at the University of Toronto, wanted to join the Canadian Army. When he came out with this, we were amazed. He would go not as a drafted soldier, but as a volunteer; we lectured him: if he pointed a rifle toward Japan, we couldn't hold our heads high; his grandparents were in Japan, so he'd have to give up the idea. The war ended just as some Nisei volunteers joined up, and since their work was interpreting, they didn't go onto the battlefield. Looking back on it now, I think we should have let our second son go, since he wanted to so much. I'm sorry to have stopped him. If he had joined the army he could have done things, such as sending money to his parents during the war, and when he came back, he could have gone to university for free.

When the order came for us to leave Mission, I was amazed. Spring had come, and we had started taking care of the fields as usual. The boxes for the strawberries had arrived. We went away in a hurry, leaving the fields and the house just as they were. Most of the Mission people, except for the ones who had gone back to Japan, applied to the B.C. Security Commission to work on sugar beet farms in Alberta. They were farmers, so they went thinking that beet growing was the best idea, and that beet prices were good, so they could make some money. They were forced to leave their land and houses behind and move. But rather than regretting it, they were resigned, I think, because Japan was at war with Canada. My husband didn't waver. He was busy taking care of the local people who were moving, and he was rushing around.

The nine of us went out, and all we were carrying were bedclothes. There were seven children, including the oldest who had just graduated from university. The youngest was old enough to start primary school. We had a piano in our house, but we donated that to the white people's church, and left our own brand-new church building behind. We got on the train, the last family to leave Mission. It was June 1942. The train passed in front of our house, and I nearly cried. But we meant to come back soon, so I didn't suffer too much.

Of course, I had to give up that idea. The government ordered our house given to returning veterans. When we were in Montreal, the government sent us $5,000 for the house and land. We used all of that for the children's education, too. I don't remember much about that time, and I don't talk about it to my husband.

When we got to the Lethbridge station, our names were called, and we were told to go to such-and-such a place. The white bosses were there to meet us with their trucks. Then the people who had come together all got separated at the station, and were taken away by their white bosses. It was just like slaves being sold off.

It was June when we got there, so the beet season was coming soon. Our whole family lived in a farmhouse, and spent one year growing beets. We got thirty cents an hour to do thinning and hoeing. It was very hard labour, absolutely the worst, and it wore me down to skin and bones. Everybody knows that farmers do physical work, but labour in the beet fields could break your back. There's no comparison with strawberry picking. The winter wasn't anything like Mission, either, what with those winds blowing from the Rockies. We got to hating Alberta, and decided to move away as soon as we could.

That was partly because the children were getting old enough for university. I understood that we couldn't move back west soon enough, so I thought it best for our children's future to go east. My husband would have done anything for the children. The most important thing in his mind was to move to a city and give the children an education. So he completely gave up the idea of going back to Mission. This was before the government order to move east, so we moved to Montreal as our oldest son wanted, at our own expense. It was unusual to move again that early. A lot of the people who went from Mission to the Lethbridge area stayed on after the war and started their own farms. They succeeded at growing potatoes and beets, and even now they're in the same area. We just keep in touch by mail.

We were in Montreal for about ten years, always looking after the children's education. The money we had all went into education. In those years, all the children got married and moved to different places. My husband became a night watchman, and worked for fifty cents an hour. This was the only work he could find in Montreal because farming was all he knew.

In 1953 we went with our second and third sons to Comber where we are now, in southwestern Ontario. My husband couldn't rest easy unless he owned some land. It was his dream to grow fruit in the Niagara area, but his brother had come before to the Comber area, and made us welcome. Our second son was out of university too, and started saying that he wanted to go into farming with his father, so we made a decision. We bought 300 acres at $200 each. It came to $60,000. At first we put in $20,000, the rest to be paid in small amounts. The times weren't good, and soy beans and wheat were cheap, so we had trouble.

Besides paying for the land, we bought big machines, fertilizer and so on, so there was a lot to handle. In the off season, we all worked like mad at whatever we could do, and for four or five years we were fixated on raising cash. I made money at home, raising 200 hens, and hogs. When we started it was 1953, and there weren't any Japanese nearby. There was still some anti-Japanese feeling, so my husband went around the neighbourhood, explaining our situation and getting everybody to approve. After that we moved in. We joined the white church right away, and tried hard to melt into the community.

Later, soy beans and wheat sold well, and we got ourselves lots of machinery, so we relaxed at last. We didn't worry about the future any more, so we left the farm to our second son and his wife, and decided to retire here ourselves. That was 10 years ago, just when our third son got married and started out on his own, and we bought this house next to his, and moved in. Around then, I visited Japan for the first time with my husband.

My family's house in Hiroshima had been completely wiped out by the atom bomb. Only my sister, living in Kyoto, lived. And as for the two of us, by living among white people, we had probably become like them, the way the government had told us to do. Well, that was probably all right. The children live in places all over the map, so we travelled here and there, visiting them. They don't give us any worry, and once a year they come to visit us here, so I'm grateful.

My third son's wife next door is a Canadian (Caucasian). She's very straightforward, and we see each other casually. She's free and easy in front of her mother-in-law, so that makes her different from the other daughters-in-law. I speak broken English, so we can't have real conversations, but we have enough to do. I see my grandchildren once a day, too. My third son has become a company worker, but he grows tomatoes and cucumbers in the greenhouse, and once in a while he works on his brother's farm.

The important thing is that both of them have good families.

When all's said and done, I can't forget how hard it was in Mission. I wonder I was able to go through with it. It's as if I wanted to praise myself. I was able to do it because of my good health. I haven't had a serious illness for these 60 years, and I've never slept in. But I also remember when we were in Alberta, it was only a year, how hard it was to keep up with everybody working on sugar beets.

I'm the thin type and maybe because I grew up in the city, I'm not strong. You need strength to be a farmer. On top of that, it's in my nature to be too thorough going into everything; I'm slow. My husband has a strong constitution and he likes farming, it suited his character. He's really crazy about farming. He says he's had a life without regrets.

It's been interesting to farm together. I got to like it, too. If I were reborn, I'd probably come to Canada and be a farmer. But I'd like to do it over with a stronger body, and a build twice as big as the one I've got.

Getting married meant a lot of expense, so if I could go without anything, why not go to Canada?

Mrs Miyo Hayashi

6 Mrs Miyo Hayashi

At an early period of settlement in Alberta, a few Japanese people founded their own small society in the southern part of the province. The first group on record is that of the several hundred Japanese who went to the Raymond area in 1908 to work in the sugar beet fields. Even earlier, perhaps, they were the workers on railway construction on the Canadian Pacific Railway, who settled in the Calgary and Lethbridge areas. It is also known that groups of Okinawans had come to work in Alberta during the heyday of coal mining.

These transplanted Japanese of the early period saved their money by working, for example, in the refineries that produced sugar from locally grown beets. Once they had amassed enough capital, they bought some land and settled on it. Although the Pacific Coast of British Columbia had a climate closely resembling Japan's, natural conditions in the neighbouring province were completely different. Winters in Alberta, when the winds from the Rockies turned into raging blizzards, gave an extreme example of the ferocity of Nature. These blizzards went on and on, and there was no knowing when they would come to an end. By the standards of Japan, half the year in Alberta consisted of winter. Since this was new territory with severe natural conditions, it is said that even experienced farmers needed four or five years to cultivate the land.

Immigrant farmers from many countries made attempts at home-steading, but few managed to settle in. Most of them, unable to endure the harsh labour and the solitude, went away. The Japanese immigrants were no exception. In summer, it was either droughts or drenching rains, over and over again. In years of heavy rain, the crops would be abundant, while in times of drought, they would be ruined. Those who watched this process repeatedly for 10 years or more, and survived, were the pioneers of the first period. Mrs Hayashi's late husband was one of the few Japanese pioneers who settled in Alberta, and indeed was one of the earlier immigrants from any country.

However, around 1920, when Mrs Hayashi got married and came to Alberta, there were already approximately 500 Japanese in the areas near towns like Lethbridge and Raymond. Almost all of them were oriented towards farming, and were hold-overs from the homesteading period. The painful efforts of these pioneers cannot be described in a few casual words. Natural conditions were only one of the problems which distinguished their experience from that of settlers on the west coast. Mrs Miyo Hayashi is typical of the wives who shared the hardships of the pioneers who surmounted life-and-death struggles.

Of the Japanese Canadians uprooted from the west coast during World War II, over 2,000 moved to Alberta, including Mrs Maki Fukushima and Mrs Tami Nakamura, the subjects of previous chapters. A good number of them stayed on after the war. To the original residents, such as the Hayashis, and the new arrivals, were added their descendants. Today, the Japanese Canadian population of southern Alberta amounts to some 2,000 people. The majority work in urban areas, but the foundation of Japanese Canadian society in Alberta was built by farmers. Success stories are said to abound among the farmers scattered here and there, who have raised their production to high levels.

Mrs Hayashi was born in March 1902, so that she is exactly 80 years old this year. There is a small town called Barnwell about 30 miles east of the city of Lethbridge, and the headquarters of the Hayashi farm are located just off the highway running through the town. Mrs Hayashi has had a cottage built for her retirement on one part of the farm, and is living there alone. Her oldest son and his family live nearby.

Her husband died about five years ago, but she has a large family of eight children, seven of them living in Alberta. Four of them are established with their families very close by. These eight children have given Mrs Hayashi 31 grandchildren, and the recent addition of three great-grandchildren has rounded out the family. Therefore, Mrs Hayashi's everyday activities revolve around family events, and they keep her very busy. Every day, someone visits her house to tell her the latest news and, after exchanging information, goes home.

Mrs Hayashi loves country life and has never been lonely just because she lives in an isolated spot. She never has a moment of boredom. In the middle of the property are a large vegetable garden and flower beds. She says that just taking care of them gives her too much work to do. She gathers and freezes enough vegetables in the summer to keep her supplied for a whole year. She is overweight, and high blood pressure makes her watch her diet, but she finds sweet things irresistible, and ends up eating too many of them. Mrs Hayashi is a champion pie-maker who has repeatedly won prizes in baking contests. Even now, out of habit, she bakes a pie once a week. She laughs, saying that if she makes pies with different fillings, someone is sure to come and get them, to take home.

Because of her savings, stored up in the course of her life alone, she has no financial wants. She feels free to go on group tours, or to go out visiting with friends. None the less, she cannot forget she is basically a farm wife, and she does not wear dressy clothes or go to restaurants. It is her habit never to be extravagant even though she has money, and she declares that this will not change to the end of her life. Her children feel for her, saying she is handicapped by her character, but Mrs Hayashi is resigned, explaining that she is a product of the Meiji era.

The most striking object in Mrs Hayashi's unpretentiously decorated living room is a photograph from her early married days, in an oval frame 50-centimetres high. Taken 60 years ago, it shows the 33-year old groom and the young bride of 21 years. This was the first time she was photographed in Western clothes since coming to Canada, and the expression of the bride, beside her self-possessed groom, is full of the determination and ardour of a young wife. The set of her mouth, showing an almost fierce resolve, gives a somehow favourable impression. I found myself suddenly moved, and realized that I had been looking intently at the portrait for some time.

If Mrs Hayashi can laugh as she tells stories of the hardships of long ago, it is no doubt because she is now comfortable, both economically and psychologically. The Hayashi family, riding the wave of postwar agricultural development in Alberta, steadily constructed and expanded their base. Mrs Hayashi participated as a producer in this process of development. Since the Hayashis were able to buy land, to settle on it, and to have raised a big family, she can say, "I think I've done what I could do, and what I should have done."

Even now, when she speaks with other people from Kagoshima Prefecture who live in nearby towns, she uses the full Kagoshima dialect which is sometimes completely obscure to people from other parts of Japan. Not only does she have a regional accent, but her speech is full of English words. For some reason, practically all her numbers, whether years or distances, are in English. When she talks about her husband's fondness for reading and how he used to read all day, she uses the English words for book and all day, and often punctuates her sentences with "I think," in a Japanese accent.

Mrs Hayashi's home town, the former village of Higashi Kokubu in Aira-gun of Kagoshima Prefecture, was one of a number of villages strung along the coast of the Okuma peninsula. Today, it forms part of the city of Kokubu, whose population is 37,000. I remembered that Mrs Hayashi had said the whole village could be seen from the top of the mountain of Shiroyama Park, and so I climbed Mount Shiroyama. First of all, there is a magnificent view of the island Sakurajima, and then you see the train running along the Okuma railway line, as well as the coastal line in the area of Shikine. A check of a map with the old place names shows that the village of Higashi Kokubu is on the railway running along the coast.

In our time, since Kokubu has become a satellite of the city of Kagoshima, a great many people leave the city in the morning, to return only at night. Outside the centre of town, nobody can be seen working on the sea or in the fields. There are only some old men by the seashore, killing time by dangling fishing lines in the water. They say it has been some time since fish could be caught in Kinko Bay. A line of houses clings to the coastline, and mountains press in from the other side at a distance from the road and the railway. The mountainsides are terraced with fields, where the farm wives do their best to grow vegetables or flowers. The weaving which Mrs Hayashi did as a young woman has disappeared, and Oshima pongee cloth is now a high-priced item of folk art. She would no doubt be astounded at the idea of such things as hand-woven pongee as a prized souvenir typical of the area, and a very expensive one at that.

The prefecture of Kagoshima was notable among others in Japan as a source of great numbers of temporary workers and other emigrants. The available arable land per farming household was minimal, compared to other prefectures, and after the decline of the fishing industry, farm families did not have enough opportunity to engage in a side business. Local histories record that every part of the prefecture saw emigrants leaving for North or South America. It is said that from an early date, a steady stream of emigrants went to North America from villages like Hayato, Ibusuki and Tarumizu, but we do not know the various reasons for their departure. Overseas emigration was evidently not concentrated in one district alone, and so the America Village phenomenon did not occur in this case.

With the 1920s, under the pressure of harsh economic times, came a rush to emigrate to Brazil or Manchuria. In this period, emigration was dealt with through prefectural governments. The records remaining in the regional offices are almost complete. Thus the accounts of overseas emigration in the prefectural histories focus on Brazil and Manchuria. However, emigration to North America was almost exclusively of the unregulated type, and was not handled by the prefecture. It is safe to say that almost nothing is known about emigration to Canada. "I'm sure Mr X.'s grandfather went overseas," said the wife of a merchant family whom I met in Shikine. But as it turned out, nobody could remember for sure whether he had gone to the United States, Canada or Brazil.

In Kagoshima, the most severely depopulated prefecture in all Japan, many people leave their home town at least once. Mrs Hayashi's eight brothers and sisters also set off on the path of temporary work elsewhere, and arrived in faraway places, some as far away as Alberta, Canada. Since they spent their last years in the lands where they went, their family home became deserted. In their native area of Southern Kagoshima, where not one of them returned, the sea and mountains are calm as ever, and offer an extreme contrast to the harshness of nature in Alberta. Human beings can survive because they can become accustomed to any place at all. I marvelled at this fact, as I thought of Mrs Hayashi, no doubt working away even now in a field in the far-off countryside of Alberta.

I was born in Higashi Kokubu in Aira-gun, Kagoshima Prefecture, and my husband was born in a place called Towa-cho about a mile away. Nowadays, they're both part of Kokubu City. In the Kokubu area they grow tobacco and it's famous for a radish called *Sakurajima daikon*. My family's house was just in front of the sea. That was Kinko Bay. From our house we could see the ocean and the big island, Sakurajima. It was a nice place as far as the climate and scenery went.

There's a 12-year age difference between my husband and me. I was born in 1902 and he was born in 1890. If he were alive he'd be over 90. About five years ago, he had a stroke and was sick for a little while before he died.

My husband came to Canada in 1906 when he was 16. His family had a big farm, but he was just a second son, so even if he'd stayed at home, he wouldn't have inherited the property. So he thought he'd go somewhere else, to a foreign country. There wasn't anybody over here to look after him, but he came with a friend. When he landed in Victoria, it was his 16th birthday, he said.

He worked five years in all kinds of places in British Columbia, such as a coal mine, and he was a schoolboy in a minister's house. At 16, he was still a child, after all. My husband grew up in this country. It seems he went to high school to study English, so he didn't have any trouble with the language. He must have done all kinds of things before he joined the army, when he was 23. For example, he came to Alberta, and worked on farms and sugar refineries near Raymond.

When he turned 23, it was 1914, and World War I broke out. He went into the Canadian Army, and was in Europe for three years. That's a picture of him as a soldier. It seems that from very early on, he intended to become a Canadian. That's why he joined the army. He said he'd heard a speech somewhere by a famous officer, and he was so moved that he decided to join up. After he came back from the war, he opened a market in Raymond, and he'd take vegetables and things to Calgary and sell them there. The money he got from sales went for food, and he didn't have anything left over.

He invested all the money he brought back from the war in potato and carrot farming, but that didn't work out. He had nothing left over. Once he had a small restaurant in Raymond, but it burnt down. He really had a hard time. One day, the manager of the E.P. Ranch in High River, which was owned by the Duke of Windsor, came to Calgary, and just by chance he got talking to my husband. He ended up asking him to work at the ranch as a cook. Since my husband had run a restaurant, he knew how to cook. So that's how he came to work on a ranch, and he settled down there for about three years. Then he went back to Japan to look for a wife. At the time, he was 33.

As for me, my father died when I was 13, and life wasn't easy for my mother and me. I was the youngest of eight, and my brothers and sisters were all working in other places. When my father was alive, he had a steamboat and went back and forth to Kagoshima City. It was transport work. There were three storehouses at my family's place, and the farmers would bring in their rice when it was ready, to leave it in the storehouse. That's what my father would take to the city. Then a railway got built from Kagoshima to the village of Hayato, so they could transport rice by train. When that happened, my family's business was finished. All of my five older brothers went to work somewhere else, and they weren't even at home when I was growing up.

I graduated from the second year of upper primary school, and went to supplementary classes for a year. Even if I'd wanted to go on to girls' school, I couldn't have. But I went right through school from first grade to second year in upper primary school. For eight years running, I won first prize, and at graduation, I got a certificate on behalf of all that year's graduates. That's why I liked school. If my father had lived, I would have gone on to a higher school. But after graduation I learned pongee weaving, and worked. Nowadays, that's very expensive material, but then there were lots of Oshima pongee companies around

Kokubu and Shikine, and they'd hire young girls to do the weaving.

I got to be a teacher of pongee weaving, and was hired by a company. I went around teaching in Shikine and towns close by and though I didn't get a lot of money, I saved some. I could sew, too, in a general way. Before I got married, I wove a bolt of pongee for my mother-in-law to be, and I made it into a kimono. That was the custom back home. After I came here, too, I liked sewing. Until a while ago, I used to make Japanese clothes for my grandchildren. But they grew up so fast and the clothes got small too soon. It was a pity.

There was talk of marriage for me from time to time. When I was going to come over here, people knew I was up for marriage, so somebody started making arrangements. Then, suddenly, my husband's name came up, because he was related to the person that was handling my marriage discussions. Since my family didn't have any money, my older brothers wanted to send me to Canada. Because if they married me off in Japan, I'd need a lot of things, and that meant a great deal of expense. So if I were to get married and go to America, all they had to do was send me over here. That's why these marriage talks came off. It's because my brothers and sisters were stingy.

My mother didn't want to see me go. I didn't want to go to Canada, either, because I'd never thought of it seriously. If I'd grown up in a well-off family, then I'd never have come to America. My husband had come back with money, so he took care of everything, all the wedding and travel expenses. They told me it was all right to get married without bringing anything, just myself, and that's how I came.

The matchmaker really worked hard telling us that this man's family was well off, they had a lot of property, mountains and fields, and that he had a good character, too. For my engagement present all I got was two sets of eight rice cakes each. In my home town the custom was, you handed out one cake each to your relatives and friends. For my trousseau, all I had was kimonos that I sewed myself, and I brought lots of those, but afterwards when we got very poor over here in Canada, I took them all apart and made Western clothes for the children.

My husband was going through a matchmaker who'd found him a bride. So he had come back to Japan thinking he'd marry her. She was a young girl in my neighbourhood, and I was friends with her. It seems that in the beginning, my husband went to see her, but she was so shy that she wouldn't come out to meet him, even though he waited all day long. So the matchmaker was in a fix, and brought him to my house, and since I was there, they suddenly started talking about my case. My husband took a liking to me as soon as we met, and it was settled right away. And so when he came to my parents' house like that, just by chance, well, it turned into a marriage meeting. It happened just at New Year's. After a month, we got married; it was February 10.

That girl they'd been thinking of, she was prettier than me, but she didn't want to get married at all, and so it worked out better with me. I didn't know much about Canada, but I'd been hearing talk about money growing on trees in America since I was a little girl, so it's not as if I'd never wanted to go. I got married without even having a real talk with my husband, and came over here in March. It was 1923, and I was 21 years old.

We took the train to Kobe from my village, and on the way I listened to my husband's stories about Canada. My husband said he was working on the E.P. Ranch, but I didn't understand any of the details. From the way he talked, he didn't seem to be having a hard time. His parents had told us to come back to Japan in three years, but I think that since he'd come to Canada when he was young, he never felt like going back to Japan from the very beginning. When we got married, too, he kept saying he thought Canada was better. He'd been in the army, so he was naturalized, and didn't feel he was in Canada just to do temporary work.

My husband turned out to be just what the matchmaker said. He had a very good nature. There was nobody like him. He treated me so well. We were together for 50 years and never had a fight. Even when things got on my nerves and I complained, he didn't say anything, he just listened, and when I got mad at the children, he'd scold me, saying I shouldn't lose my temper at them. He was a gentle person, and very quiet. He didn't talk a lot, but he'd read books from morning to night. I'm the opposite type; if I read a book for ten minutes it gives me a headache.

My husband had come to Japan with a Canadian passport, and that was unusual in those days. When I got married, my name went into the passport, and that's how I came over. At the immigration office in Kobe, we were told by a lower officer: "You're just a couple of Japanese, you think you're smart, don't you, going back on a Canadian passport?" but a higher officer came and said, "Never mind, you're all right," and so we could come to Canada. My husband took me on a boat called the *Hawaii Maru*, and it took 14 days to make the crossing. Up to then I'd been wearing Japanese clothes, but in Victoria he bought me Western ones. That's a picture of me over there, wearing those clothes. It's our wedding picture, taken in Calgary. I was wearing a navy suit with a white blouse, and a necklace. That was the first time I'd worn anything like that. I had a whole outfit, with a coat, a hat and a pair of boots.

We had about ten days of holidays in Vancouver, and then we got on the train to Calgary. Then we took another rest to do some shopping and so on, then we went to High River. In those days, High River was just a little station. We rode in a buggy for 27 miles to get to the E.P. Ranch. We'd come from Vancouver, it was a lively place, and even Calgary was all right, but when we were riding in the buggy, all of a sudden we came to such a lonely spot, and I didn't know what kind of a faraway, lonesome place I would be taken to, and I cried all the rest of the way.

I saw houses here and there, but they were all funny looking, just like chicken coops made a little bigger. That was the first time I thought I shouldn't have come to such a place, and I kept bawling. My husband just looked at me out of the corner of his eye, and afterwards he used to tell people about it, he said he didn't know to make me feel better. I just couldn't stop crying. Though I did feel relieved when we got to the ranch and I saw a beautiful house, and a nice log cabin for us to live in. Later, when there was shopping to do, or when the Stampede was on, I'd get taken to Calgary, so I didn't feel lonely at all. But I've never forgotten how I cried during that first buggy ride.

We worked at the E.P. Ranch for three years. My husband was the cook and I was the housekeeper. Nowadays, that ranch has changed hands, and there's nothing left to make you think of that time. It used to belong to the Prince of Wales, and he would come in the summer. All kinds of people came along with him. They'd bring lots of different things, from whisky to cookies. When visitors came, there'd be parties, and it was fun. In those days I'd learned a good deal of English, and spoke it all the time. Near the ranch there was a river where my husband used to catch trout. He'd bring them home to cook; everybody would eat the trout saying how good it was.

The manager was a very fine man, and he was educated. That ranch had a lot of horses and cattle, and my husband would put the cattle on a truck and take them away to be sold, so he wasn't just a cook. Anyway, the boss liked him. Even after we left the ranch three years later, and we'd gone to Welling, he came to see us three times, trying to get us back. We thought of my husband's younger brother, since he was in Vancouver and still single, and sent him to the ranch instead, but he didn't work out. Even brothers can be very different from each other.

The year after I came to Canada, at New Year's, my oldest son was born. We had three children in three years, two at the ranch, and I was carrying the third when we left. It was embarrassing because I'd had a baby every year for three years. I was always ashamed to work in the house with a big stomach, so I started to say I wanted to leave the ranch. My husband thought the ranch wasn't a good place to bring up children, so we decided to go into farming together. He had farming experience, and he thought it would be better for the children's future. In Alberta, in the old days, that was almost the only work we could have done anyway. We rented 35 acres in Welling from a man called Mr Wilde and moved to a place where there was nothing but a miserable-looking house. That was in 1926.

Welling is on the road from Lethbridge, on a corner where you turn off to go to Raymond. The house we lived in is gone, and there's a new building on the lot. The land had to be irrigated, and besides wheat we grew potatoes, beets, carrots, cabbage—vegetables like that. We were really poor in those days and we suffered. I can't tell you how much worse it was than if we'd stayed on the ranch. We were so poor I can't put it into words. We had seven more children, about two years apart from each other. One died right after being born and another one, the smartest, died in an accident at the age of eleven.

We did well the year we moved, but soon the Depression hit, and we had a terrible time. Everything went wrong. Prices went down; a 100-pound sack of potatoes was five dollars, a bushel of wheat was 19 cents, and even so they didn't sell. Everybody was in debt. We didn't pay taxes for two or three years, and we were at the end of our rope. For years we couldn't feed the children rice, and it was really pitiful.

We didn't have any luck with the weather, either. It was dry all the time, so it wasn't good for the crops, and sometimes it rained so much the potatoes rotted and we couldn't get any seedlings. Even so we went into the fields every day, and tried to grow what we could. We'd pick potatoes and vegetables and store them in the cellar. We put them in bags to sell, and took them to the train station. The children did the same as we did from the time they were little, and helped us a lot. When my husband went out at night to water the fields, they didn't have to be told, they went with him.

In the winter I'd put the children to bed, then go down to the cellar with my husband to put the potatoes into sacks. When there was an order he couldn't manage by himself; I used to help. We'd choose the potatoes, put them into hundred-pound sacks and send them out. During the dry spells, the potatoes would get lumps on them, and they didn't look good, so we couldn't sell them at a high price. If it rained too much, they'd rot. So potato-growing was hard. If there was no crop, we'd be in even worse trouble, and my husband would work at anything. He'd go out to be a cook at some farm nearby, or work in a coal mine. That's how he provided for the family.

Our oldest son wasn't strong, and was sick in hospital for a year, but we couldn't pay for the bus fare to the Lethbridge hospital. At first, he was going to see a doctor in Raymond, but he wasn't properly looked after. He got thin, down to skin and bones, and we gave up, thinking he was a goner. They found there was water stored up in his body, and put him into the Lethbridge hospital. Needless to say, we didn't have enough money to put him in hospital, let alone buy him something nice to eat.

Whenever I wanted to visit the hospital, I'd stand at an intersection and put up my hand to hitchhike. When I think of it now, I start to cry. Thank goodness somebody would always come by and pick me up. To get back, too, there was always some nice person to give me a ride. One dollar would have done for the bus ride, but I didn't even have that dollar. We had no cash at all. One of the children came to me once and said: "Mama, somebody gave me a half-dollar," and something like that would make us happy.

That whole area was "Mormontown," and the Mormon church was good to us. When they made Christmas cakes to sell at bazaars, I'd get asked to bake too. They sold tickets at a quarter each, and when they got the money for the cakes, they gave me everything they'd collected. At the party afterwards, they'd put all the money for my baking in a bag, and give it to me as a Christmas present. I'd start crying then, and I couldn't stop.

There's a store in Raymond run by Mormons, it's called the Mercantile, and we used to charge everything we bought there. They'd trust us for a long time, without charging interest. At the end of the year, no matter how hard it was, we'd pay off a little, but we simply couldn't manage to pay off a whole year's debt. Every year, the debts would build up. Looking back on it, I wonder how they ever lent us that much. But if we're sincere about what we do, then the other person is going to do well by us. Even now, I'm grateful to that store.

What with the Depression and the drought coming on top of each other, all the farms were in trouble, and in the end we couldn't manage to feed the children any rice. We did have potatoes, but no money to buy rice. There was a big meeting at the Japanese Association in Raymond, that almost all the 40 families belonged to; the Buddhist Church was at the centre of it. They talked about going to Manchuria. Somebody said, things aren't working out here, so how about us going to Manchuria in a group? A representative was going to Vancouver anyway, so he stopped off at the Japanese Consulate and asked how things were over there. They told him the Depression had hit everywhere, and just at that time, the Manchurian Incident had happened, so that was the end of that idea. We were in real trouble, so much that we were seriously thinking of getting out of Alberta.

If you got sick and had to see a doctor, you couldn't pay the bill. When I had my babies, I never had a doctor. My oldest son and daughter were born on the ranch, so a nurse helped me out. On the farm, I never saw a doctor even though I knew I was pregnant, and my husband always delivered the babies. So all of them were born at home.

To get the bed ready for the birth, I used to sew together some cloth I'd brought from Japan, then sit on it to have the baby. I made a crib out of our old wicker trunks, and got the small things ready. I'd read Japanese magazines like *The Housewife's Companion*, and that's how I knew what childbirth was about. My second son was born at home too, but in that case he had a twin, who died right after birth. When I was pregnant I didn't know it was going to be twins. The neighbour came to help, but she'd never had a baby, so she was just amazed, and she couldn't deliver the child. She went and called my husband, and got him to cut the umbilical cord. I was the one who gave the babies their first bath, too. I had the other children to look after, so I couldn't stay in bed for even a week. My husband helped out a bit, but I used to get up in a week and do the laundry.

Some women died in childbirth, but I had a strong constitution. I never had a difficult birth, and I had ten babies with no problems. I didn't know anything about birth control, and my husband wanted a lot of children too. He used to be glad, saying, "Oh, another one!" These days people only have one or two. I wonder why they limit themselves. Because there's no reason they shouldn't be born.

All the children grew up and went to school in Welling, except for the youngest one who was born after we came here to Barnwell. The school was more than two miles from home, so we sent them by bike. In winter they walked to school, so the children remember some hard times, too. When five of them were going to school, I'd send them off with a lunch of home-baked bread. As my husband had been a cook, I learned how to make bread and pies. About twice every week I baked six ordinary loaves, and then some "two-pound bread," loaves that took two pounds of flour to make. Even at that, it wasn't enough sometimes. I wonder now how I could have fed all those children and brought them up. My husband kept saying the children had to get through school, and I think the children did well to go.

When I didn't have to work in the fields, I was busy sewing and mending. Anyway, we'd had eight children one after the other, so I was always doing patchwork on overalls and stockings. I'd patch, and mend, and mend over again. In winter we'd have days in a row when the wind was so strong you couldn't go out. At times like that we'd be shut up indoors, with the children as company. The winter was so long that a lot of women would get a local disease, goitres. It was a kind of nervous disease, where the thyroid glands would swell. In a place like this, people with weak nerves can't put up with things, whether they're men or women. I was lucky to be so busy, there was no time to be sick.

168   Picture Brides

When we were still in Welling, the war began. What I felt wasn't so much shock, but disgust. From the beginning, I was against the war, that is against Japan going to war, because we owned land, and we'd settled down on it. People who weren't farmers couldn't put up with it. The people who stayed on were all farmers, and naturalized Canadians. And my husband had even joined the army in the First World War, so he couldn't be moved at all, saying it was proper to be completely loyal to Canada.

It's strange to say "thanks to the war," but the price of potatoes went up all of a sudden. It was amazing. We took in three carloads and, with a 100-pound sack selling for $50, made $1,000. The price went up by 5 or 10 times. The price of wheat went up, too, and the year after the war began, we had made money, so we could save. In the Barnwell area around here, one acre of land costs $1,000 or $2,000 now, but when we got here in 1943, one acre cost $50. A quarter section, that is, one division of 160 acres, was $8,000, and we paid one half when we came or $4,000. Sugar beets were $10 a ton, so we made $1,000 for 100 tons, and by paying $1,000 every year, we ended up owning a quarter section in four years. It happened really fast.

This land we're living on now, they used to grow wheat on it. But wheat doesn't need soil preparation. It was a February when we came to look at it, and because of the snow we couldn't see it. But when spring came, we saw it was rough land with nothing but stones. A neighbour woman advised us: "This is a terrible place, so you should get out." But we'd made our down payment, so we couldn't very well leave even if we wanted to.

While we were planting potatoes, I kept picking up stones. I thought that no matter what happened, we had to take in a crop, so I worked till midnight. The stones we picked up made mountains, it looked like. Little by little we made ditches and put water through for irrigation. That made for some good fields. Potatoes grew in it well, and we got a good crop every year. From that time on, things kept getting better and better. We hadn't expected this, but it improved: luck finally came around to our side. In wartime there was a sugar shortage, so we kept getting told to produce more sugar beets, and when we did, we got good prices.

Even in wartime, there wasn't any anti-Japanese feeling in this area. The Japanese were all farmers, that's why. This area is very hard to open up, so it's a place where people really put a value on land. The ones who value land the most are the Japanese. That's why it was good for us. The white people in Raymond didn't say anything. Although the Mounties did come to town and look around to see if any Japanese were getting together on the street, and maybe talking about things they shouldn't.

At the Japanese Association, they would get small amounts of money together and contribute to the Red Cross to show that the Japanese were loyal—that's how they were cooperating with the war effort. Then people got sent from British Columbia, so that meant more Japanese around. Even then there wasn't any anti-Japanese feeling. The BC people stayed for a while at the Buddhist Church until they found work, and then they went to work on sugar beet farms. Some Kagoshima people came to work on our farm too, and lived with us for a year or so. In those days there weren't any machines for thinning sugar beets, it had to be done by hand. So they must have found it was very tough work. They all worked hard, though.

One of the BC people was a Kagoshima man, Reverend K, a United Church minister, and he went around preaching to the Japanese. The Japanese around here were Buddhists, and they were a solid group, so Reverend K hadn't just come to an inconvenient place to live, he also had a hard time trying to win over some stubborn people. My husband and I didn't have any religion to speak of, but in Welling, we belonged to the Buddhist Church. But then we met Reverend K. He was evangelizing, and first my husband got enthusiastic about it, and though he'd never read the Bible before, he started to study Christianity.

It got to the point where the reverend would get people together and start a study group, or go out here and there and make speeches to people. By and by he got some converts, and everybody put in some money to buy a car for the minister, so he could go around spreading the Gospel. The year the war ended, my husband was going to be baptized. I didn't intend to get baptized myself, I just went along and sat beside him. Then, my husband said, "You stand up too, and say the pledge with me," so all of a sudden, with no preparation at all, I became a Christian.

I'd converted by chance, and for a while I suffered. All of the people I was friendly with belonged to the Buddhist Church, and I was a member too, but as I learned to pray in the Christian religion, my bad feelings went away little by little. We had a Buddhist altar for my dead son, and I was wondering what to do with it, when luckily some people came along who wanted an altar and I gave it to them. My husband was very serious about his religion, so all I had to do was follow along behind him.

When we were in Welling, we sent the children to the Mormon church, not the Buddhist one. Because it's Mormontown around here. The church is just beside the school. In school, too, they taught Mormonism once a week, so if some children didn't go to church with everybody else, they got shunned. So the children kept going to the Mormon church all along. Some have come to be very serious believers, and others haven't. My oldest son, for example, is a good Mormon. He went to Japan as a missionary, and he gives one-tenth of his earnings to the Church.

The Buddhists would say snide things, like, "That church is very good at doing service, isn't it." They didn't know anything about the church's doctrines, but they'd say things like, "Polygamy is barbaric." But myself, when I was in trouble, I got a lot of help from that church, so I haven't a thing to say against it. They've treated me very well.

The young Mormons go to California or Japan as missionaries. The men go for two years, and the women for one and a half, and they learn to do service by being missionaries. The church headquarters pays for the travel expenses, but the parents take care of the monthly support. If the parents aren't enthusiastic about it, they can't do mission work. One of my grandchildren became a strong believer and went to Japan for mission work. He got good at Japanese and wrote me letters, and says it would be nice to go back.

The Mormon church is getting stronger and stronger. There's a big church in Barnwell, too. My oldest son and his family are members. It seems that every Sunday so many people come to worship that they can hardly fit into the church. My husband and I didn't become Mormons. After the war we were United Church, and we really worked to build the church in Taber. Since I came here and became a Christian by chance, and things got better every year, I believe it's by the grace of God, and I'm grateful.

Farmers work with nature, after all. I used to pray for the crops. And when I did, my prayers were heard, and things got better and better. We bought a machine called the International to do the beet thinning for the first time, and we bought a potato digger too. We were the first around here to buy one. And every year we added to our land. We only had 100 acres of potatoes at first, but every year we added, and now we've got approximately 1,000 acres.

When my husband was 70, he had a bad accident with an onion harvester and lost his right hand and couldn't work any more. He was still healthy but had to retire. He turned everything over to the children. My husband was somebody who would keep things to himself even when he had something to say, but the children have a lot of spirit, so they're doing well. They've been really good to us. My oldest son and fifth son, and my oldest daughter's husband, the three of them have set up a company. The others have gone here and there, doing different things. All three girls have jobs, and they're working. The eight of them get along well.

Even after my husband retired, I kept helping on the farm. I'd pack potatoes and onions, and work all through the season. I've liked working outside since I was young, you see. My people weren't farmers back in Japan, but I liked it. Whenever the relatives were doing things like rice planting, I used to go and help.

I don't like to sit around doing nothing. That's why I grew vegetables around this house and sold them. Now that the children won't let me, I can't grow much. The vegetables get bought by people who've been coming for a long time, so I just sell what I grow.

I sold fresh beans and asparagus and made good money. I saved that money little by little and got interest on it. As the saying goes in Japanese, little specks of dust pile up to make a mountain. When I reported the money on my income tax form, the government came around once asking how I could have made so much. I explained that this was money I'd saved up little by little by working every year for 40 years, and that satisfied them.

When you plant crops, or harvest them on 1,000 acres, it's a terrific amount of work. Nowadays there's machines for everything: digging, sowing, planting, and it isn't that much trouble. We've bought our machinery on borrowed money, so it seems there isn't much left after the debt is paid off. We grow 1,000 acres of wheat, and about the same amount of sugar beets too. Then we raise 1,500 head of cattle, and as for feed, we get some from our vegetables, and wheat and hay become feed for the cattle, so it goes towards the feed money. The feed money is nothing to sneeze at. The vegetables, they're washed at the plant, and frozen and packed to send to markets in BC. A lot of people come to work at the plant, take care of the cattle, and work on the crops, and that is a big expense, too. Farmers are always saying they don't make money; it's a game of now you see it, now you don't. The companies have trouble managing, too.

In the old days, people in Alberta were really poor. They built their own houses, flat-top buildings like chicken coops. In lots of places you lighted coal oil in lamps, and the water didn't flow out well. So it was very hard for the people who lived on farms in those days. Nowadays, wherever you go, you see nice houses and they're just like the ones in town. The farmers these days don't like living far away. They live in town and drive back and forth to do their work. They say it's for the sake of the children's education, but the way they live is extravagant. They all act like that, so they must have money. And they don't work on Sundays even at crop time, no matter how busy it is. For us, it's just unbelievable.

The Indians, they want to take Saturdays off. They don't work on rainy days, either. The cottages you see here and there are Indian houses. A lot of Indians work in this area. Around March, whole families come from Saskatchewan to work. They send their children to school around here, and in winter they close up their houses to go back to Saskatchewan. I've never asked if they have their own houses on a reserve somewhere. They come here every year, without fail. They're not dissatisfied to do the same thing year after year, you see.

It's the sixth year since my husband died. Before the war we couldn't go to Japan, not even once, but we went in 1958. It was the first time in 36 years, and since then I've been back four times. My family over there died out with my mother. My brothers and sisters have all died in other places, and now I don't have any relatives left in Japan, so what I enjoy most is seeing my old classmates. When I see them, we talk all night. We sing the old songs we learned in primary school, and we all laugh and cry, and make a lot of noise.

When we were poor I had a hard time, with all those children on my hands. I really know what it is to be poor, so I can't be extravagant; it's impossible. Even though I've got money there's nothing I want. My pocket money, I spend it to make the grandchildren happy. I've decided when my grandchildren get married, I'll buy each of them $1,000 worth of presents. This summer is like every year; three of them are getting married. But I probably can't stay alive until all 31 of them are taken care of. Maybe I can stay alive till half of them are married. The year before last, one of my granddaughters had a baby, and that was my first great-grandchild, but this year, two more were born.

The government gives everybody a $200-a-month pension. I can't spend all of mine, the way I am now. I have my own house and live alone, and my oldest son looks after all my expenses. I have pocket money, so I can't spend all of my pension money.

    I think that all in all, I've had good luck. My husband was a fine man, and I had ten children. Eight of them have grown up and they're all doing well. I'm glad I got married to come to Canada. If I'd married in Japan and stayed there, I would probably have been a widow sooner. If I'd married the man they were considering for me when I met my husband, I would have been a widow 40 years ago. When I went back to Japan in 1958 he was already dead. He'd gone to the war, and he never came back.

Afterword

The first draft of this manuscript was finished three years ago, but just at that time, I was forced to leave Toronto because of my work. I didn't have any more time to chat with the ladies, so I filed the manuscript away and time passed.

For the sake of my work, I found myself living in the middle of the great Canadian prairies, in a town so small it was almost imperceptible, completely surrounded by wheat fields. In retrospect, though, it was a good experience. I came to appreciate the newness of the west, hardly a hundred years after it was opened up by European settlers, and to experience its long, severe winters.

That was where I met Mrs Miyo Hayashi, who appears in the last chapter of this book. Her deeply-wrinkled, earth-colored skin belonged indeed to a frontier farmer. It was like seeing a delicate flower from Japan. They say that, in her youth she was pretty as well as strong-minded. She had miraculously put down roots in this region where grass and trees, let alone farm produce, were unlikely to grow.

To while away the boredom of small-town life, I took up the manuscript again. I decided to add a chapter on Mrs Hayashi and to revise the others. For some time, I had wanted to visit the home towns of these women, which happened to be emigrant villages. I seized the occasion to do research, and I went from village to village in Japan. I think this trip was a sort of sentimental journey for me, because I was now an immigrant like them.

Two years later I was able to return to Toronto, and to renew my acquaintance with the women. My greatest joy was to find all five alive. When I heard them complaining repeatedly: "It's gotten so I can't do anything any more," I felt a surge of gratitude that is all the more intense because they were still alive. I pray they will carry on bravely until the end.

While preparing this book for publication, I received the unstinting support and cooperation of Mr Shunsuke Omi of the Miraisha Publishing Company. To him I express my deepest appreciation.

Tomoko Makabe
Toronto, 1983

Further Reading

Books in English

Adachi, Ken. *The Enemy that Never Was: A History of the Japanese Canadians.* Toronto, Ont: McClelland and Stewart, 1976.
Broadfoot, Barry. *Years of Sorrow, Years of Shame: The Story of the Japanese Canadians in World War II.* Don Mills, Ont: Paperjacks, 1979.
Japanese Canadian Centennial Society. *A Dream of Riches: The Japanese Canadians, 1877-1977.* Vancouver, B.C.: Japanese Canadian Centennial Society, 1977.
Kitagawa, Muriel. *This is My Own.* Vancouver, B.C.: Talonbooks, 1985.
Knight, Rolf and Maya Koizumi. *A Man of Our Times: The Life-history of a Japanese-Canadian Fisherman.* Vancouver, B.C.: New Star Books, 1976.
Kogawa, Joy. *Obasan.* Toronto, Ont: Lester & Orpen Dennys, 1981.
La Violette, Forest E. *The Canadian Japanese and World War II.* Toronto, Ont: University of Toronto Press, 1948.
Makabe, Tomoko. "Ethnic Group Identity: Canadian-born Japanese in Metropolitan Toronto." Toronto, Ont: University of Toronto, PhD thesis, 1976.
Nakano, Takeo Ujo and Leatrice Nakano. *Within the Barbed Wire Fence: A Japanese Man's Account of His Internment in Canada.* Toronto, Ont: University of Toronto Press, 1980.

Nakayama, Gordon G. *Issei: Stories of Japanese Canadian Pioneers*. Toronto, Ont: Britannia Printers Ltd., 1983.

Oiwa, Keibo. *Stone Voices—Wartime Writings of Japanese Canadian Issei*. Montreal, P.Q.: Vehicule Press, 1991.

Omatsu, Maryka. *Bittersweet Passage*. Toronto, Ont: Between the Lines, 1993.

Shimizu, Yon. *The Exiles*. Wallaceburg, Ont: Shimizu Consulting and Publishing, 1993.

Sugimoto, Howard H. *Japanese Immigration, the Vancouver Riots and Canadian Diplomacy*. New York, N.Y.: Arno Press, 1978.

Sunahara, Ann Gomer. *The Politics of Racism: The Uprooting of Japanese Canadians During the Second World War*. Toronto, Ont: J. Lorimer, 1981.

Takashima, Shizuye. *A Child in Prison Camp*. Montreal, P.Q.: Tundra Books, 1971.

Takata, Toyo. *Nikkei Legacy—The Story of Japanese Canadians from Settlement to Today*. Toronto, Ont: NC Press Ltd, 1983.

Ward, William Peter. *White Canada Forever*. Montreal, P.Q.: McGill-Queen's University Press, 1978.

Young, C. H., R. Y. Reid and W. A. Carrothers. *The Japanese Canadians*. Toronto, Ont: University of Toronto Press, 1938.

Books in Japanese

Gamo, Masao et al. *Umi o watatta Nihon no mura (The Japanese Village that Crossed the Sea)*. Tokyo: Chuo Koron, 1962.

Hayashi, Rintaro. *Kuroshio no hate ni (At the End of the Black Current)*. Tokyo: Nichibo Shuppan, 1974.

Ito, Kazuo. *Hokubei hyakunen-zakura (A Hundred Years of*

Japanese Immigration to North America). Tokyo: Nichibo Shuppan, revised and continued, 1969.

Kudo, Miyoko. *Shakonsai—Hanayome wa ichimai no miai shashin wo te ni umi o watatte itta (Picture Brides: They Crossed the Ocean, Photograph in Hand)*. Tokyo: Domesu Shuppan, 1993.

Miyazaki, Koichiro. *Imin. Akeyuku hyakunen (Towards the Dawn: One Hundred Years of Japanese Immigration)*. Montreal, P.Q.: published by author, 1974.

Mori, Kenzo and Takami, Hiroto. *Kanada Manzo monogatari (The Story of Manzo Nagano in Canada)*. Toronto, Ont: New Canadian, 1977.

Morita, Katsuyoshi. *Paueru-gai monogatari - Kanada de kurashita rokuju-nen (Tales of Powell Street: Sixty Years of Life in Canada)*. Vancouver, B.C.: Live Canada, 1986.

Nakayama, Gordon Goichi. *Issei—Nikkei Kanadajin kaitakusha monogatari (Issei: Stories of Japanese Canadian Pioneers)*. Tokyo: Seiai Kanko Iinkai, 1987.

Nakayama, Jinshiro. *Kanada doho hatten taikan (Encyclopedia of the Development of the Japanese in Canada)*. Tokyo, 1921.

Sato, Tsutae and Sato, Hanako. *Kodomo to tomo ni gojunen—Kanada nikkei kyoiku shiki (Fifty Years with Children: A Personal Account of Japanese Canadian Education)*. Tokyo: Nichibo Shuppan, 1969.

Shimpo, Mitsuru. *Ishi o mote owaruru gotoku (As if Pursued by a Stone)*. Toronto, Ont: Tairiku Jiho, 1975.

Shimpo, Mitsuru. *Jinshu sabetsu to henken (Racial Discrimination and Prejudice)*. Tokyo: Iwanami Shoten, 1972.

Shimpo, Mitsuru. *Nihon no imin—Nikkei Kanadajin ni mirareta haiseki to tekio (Japanese Immigrants: Exclusion and Adaptation Seen in Japanese Canadians)*. Tokyo: Hyoronsha, 1977.

Tairiku Nipposha (*Continental Times*). "Kanada doho hattenshi" ("History of the Development of the Japanese in

Canada"). Vols. 1-3 Vancouver, B.C.: Tairiku Nippo Company, 1924.

Takata, Mitsuko, *Toki tabiji no koe* (*Voices from a Journey Far Away*) Tokyo: Asahi shimbun, 1990).

Tsuji, Shin'ichi, *Nikkei Kanada-jin* (*The Japanese Canadians*) Tokyo: Shobunsha, 1990).

Tsurumi, Kazuko, *Sutebuston monogatari* (*The Steveston Story*) Tokyo: Chuo Koron, 1962).

Ethnocultural Voices Series

A Black Man's Toronto, 1914-1980: the Reminiscences of Harry Gairey, edited by Donna Hill

Between Two Worlds: the Autobiography of Stanley Frolick, edited by Lubomyr Luciuk and Marco Carynnyk

The Gordon C. Eby Diaries, 1911-1913: Chronicles of a Mennonite Farmer, edited by James M. Nyce

Heroes of Their Day: the Reminiscences of Bohdan Panchuk, edited by Lubomyr Luciuk

The Finnish Baker's Daughters, by Ali Grönlund Schneider

The Memoirs of Giovanni Veltri, edited by John Potestio

An Ordinary Woman in Extraordinary Times, by Ibolya (Szalai) Grossman

Unhappy Rebel: the Life and Times of Andy Stritof, by Cvetka Kocjancic

Marynia, Don't Cry: Memoirs of Two Polish-Canadian Families, by Apolonja Maria Kojder and Barbara Głogowska

Safe Haven: the Refugee Experience of Five Families, edited by Elizabeth McLuhan

Picture Brides: Japanese Women in Canada, by Tomoko Makabe